This coloring book belongs to :

____

____

____

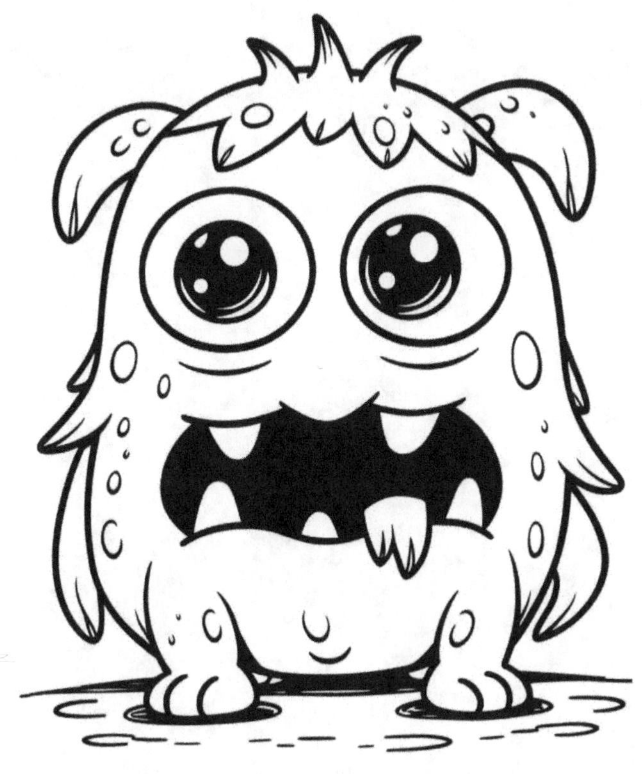

Bubblesnoot

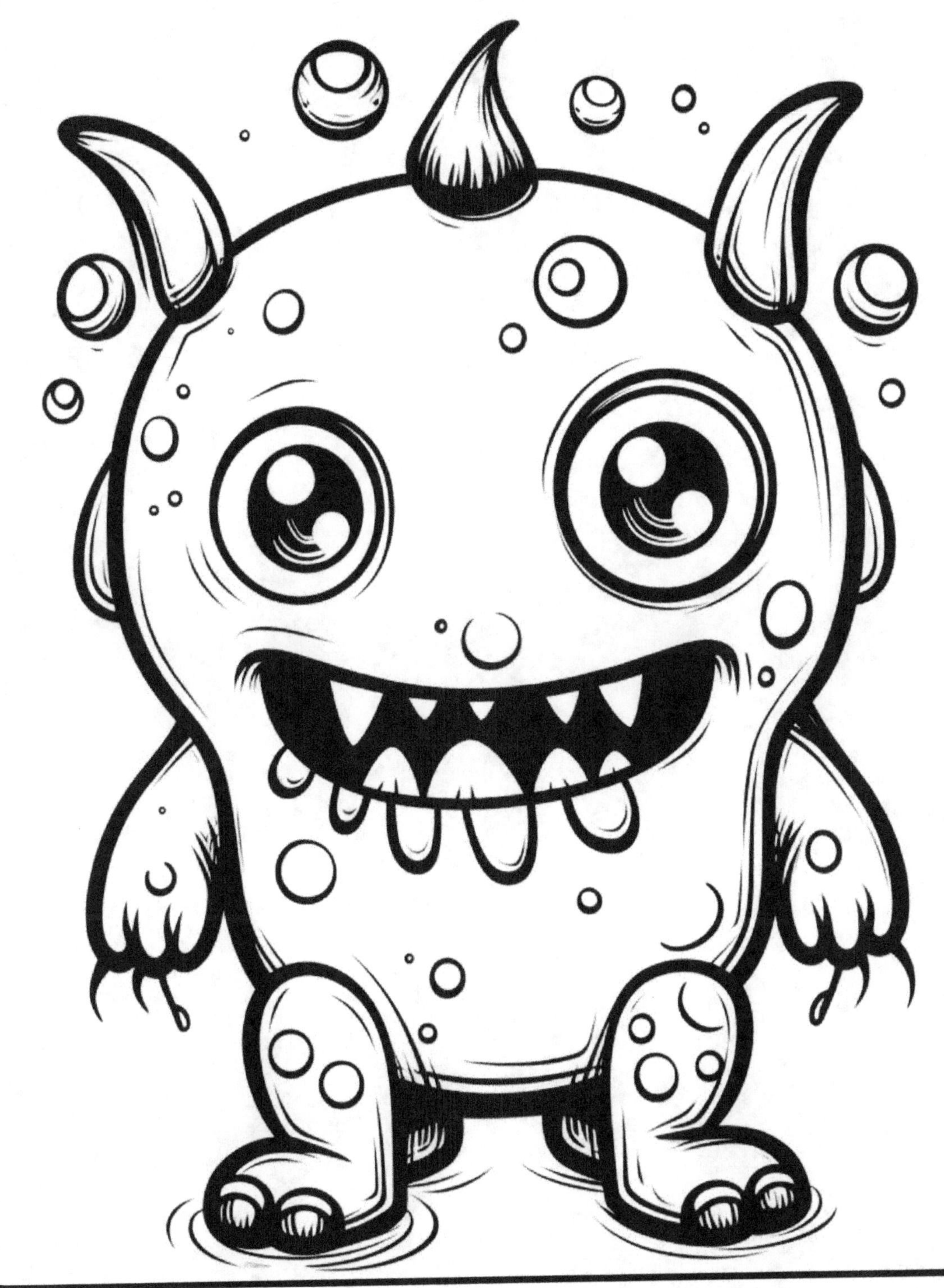

Snuggletooth

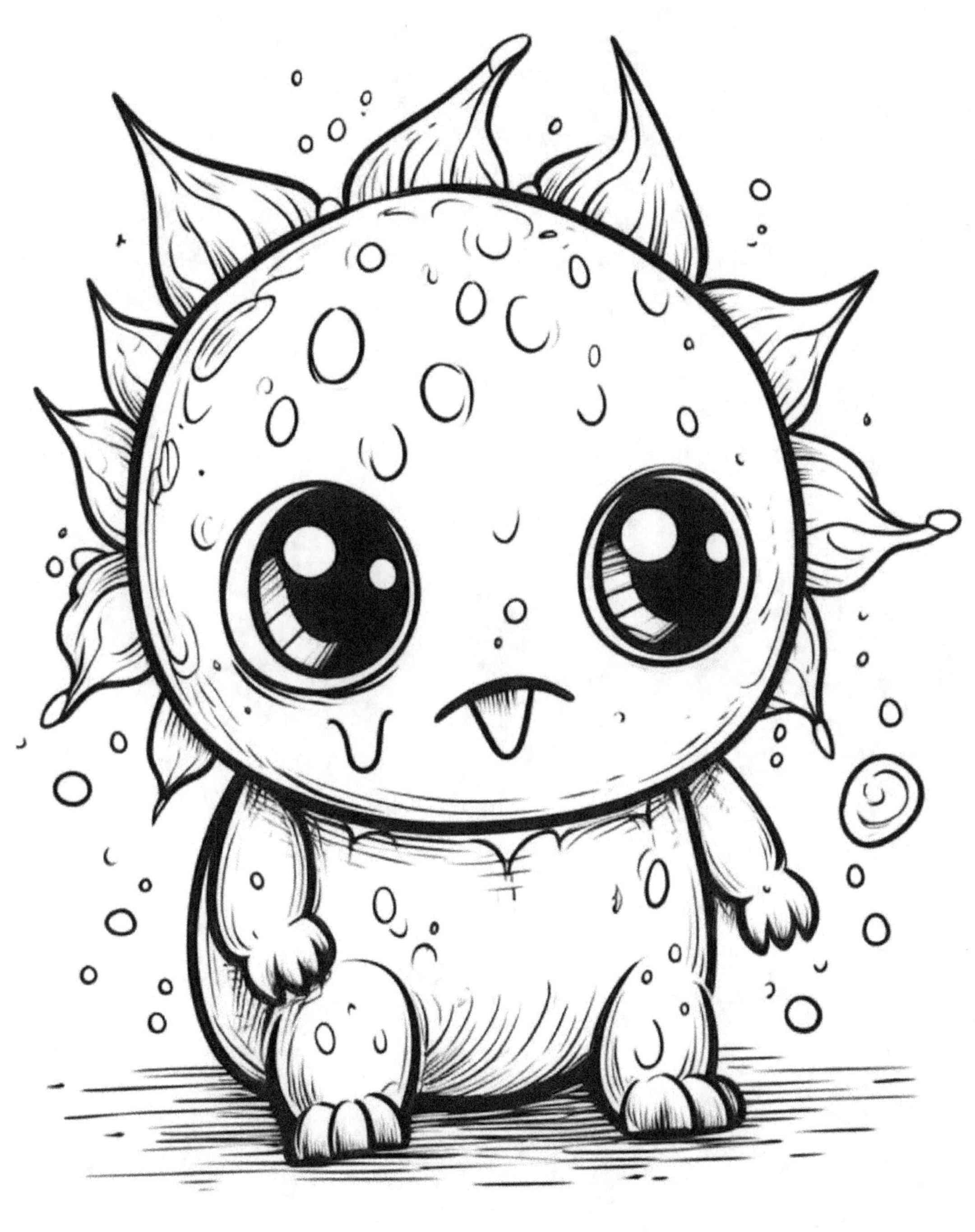

Gigglesnack

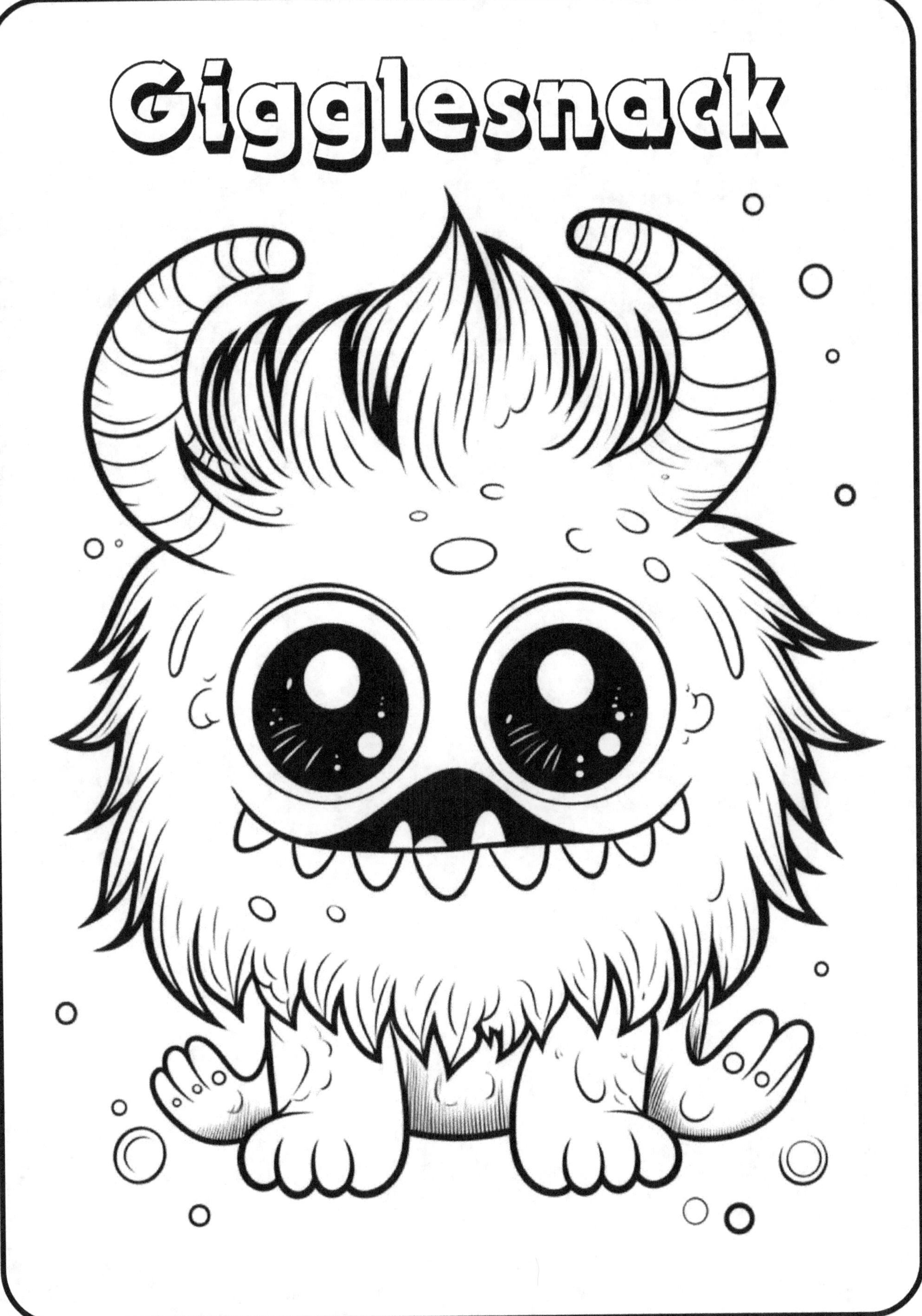

Dimplewhisk

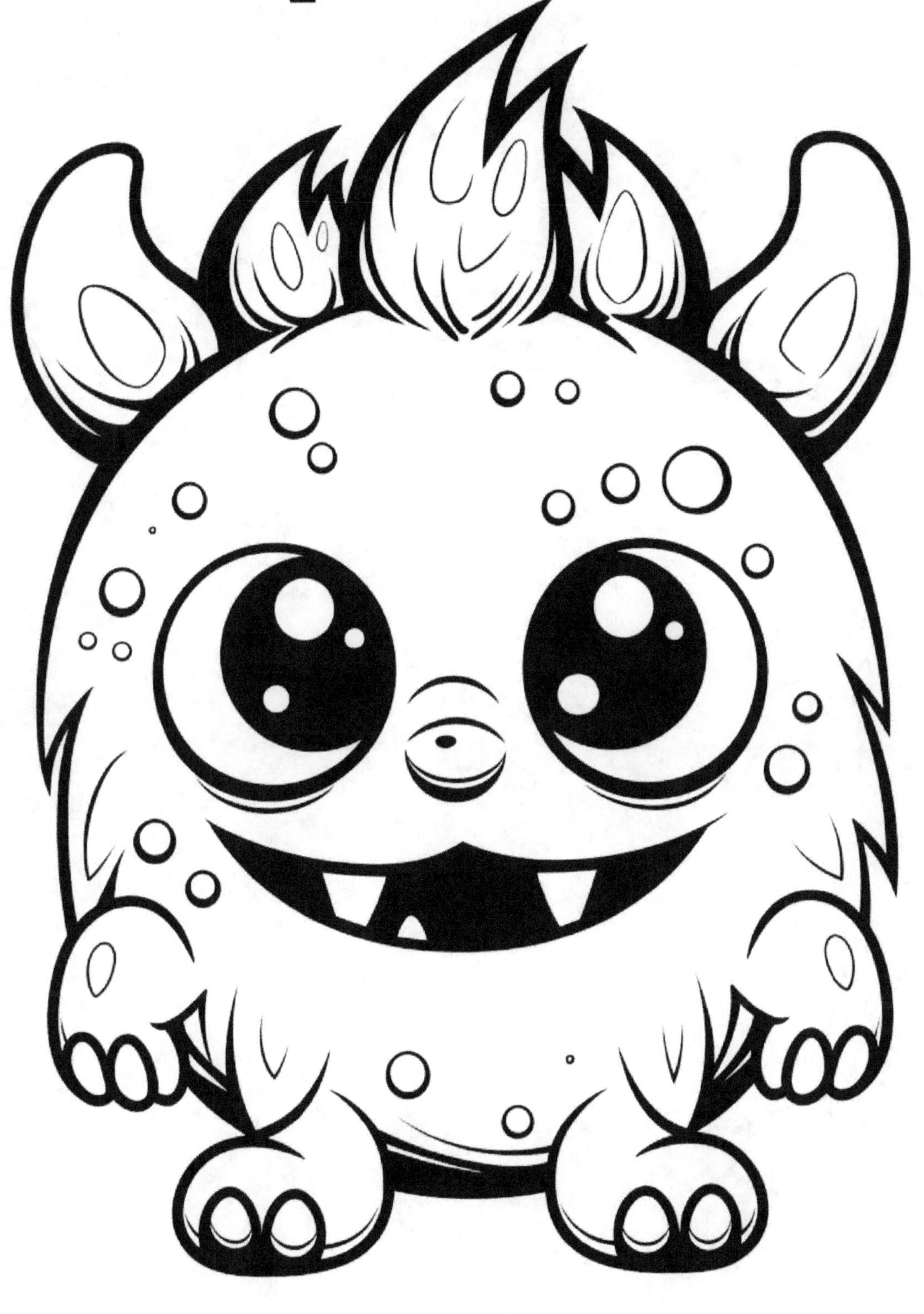

Cuddlepuff

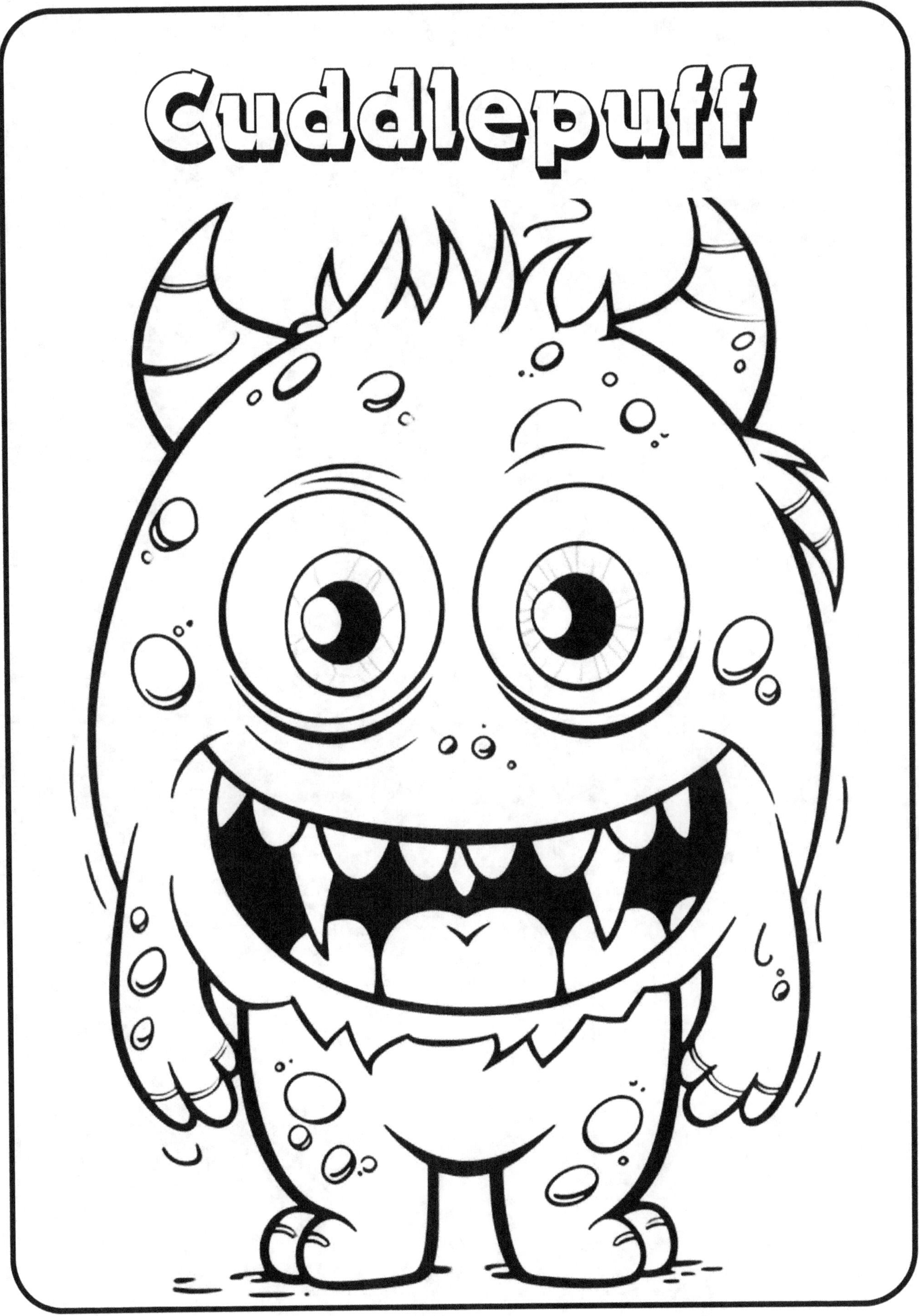

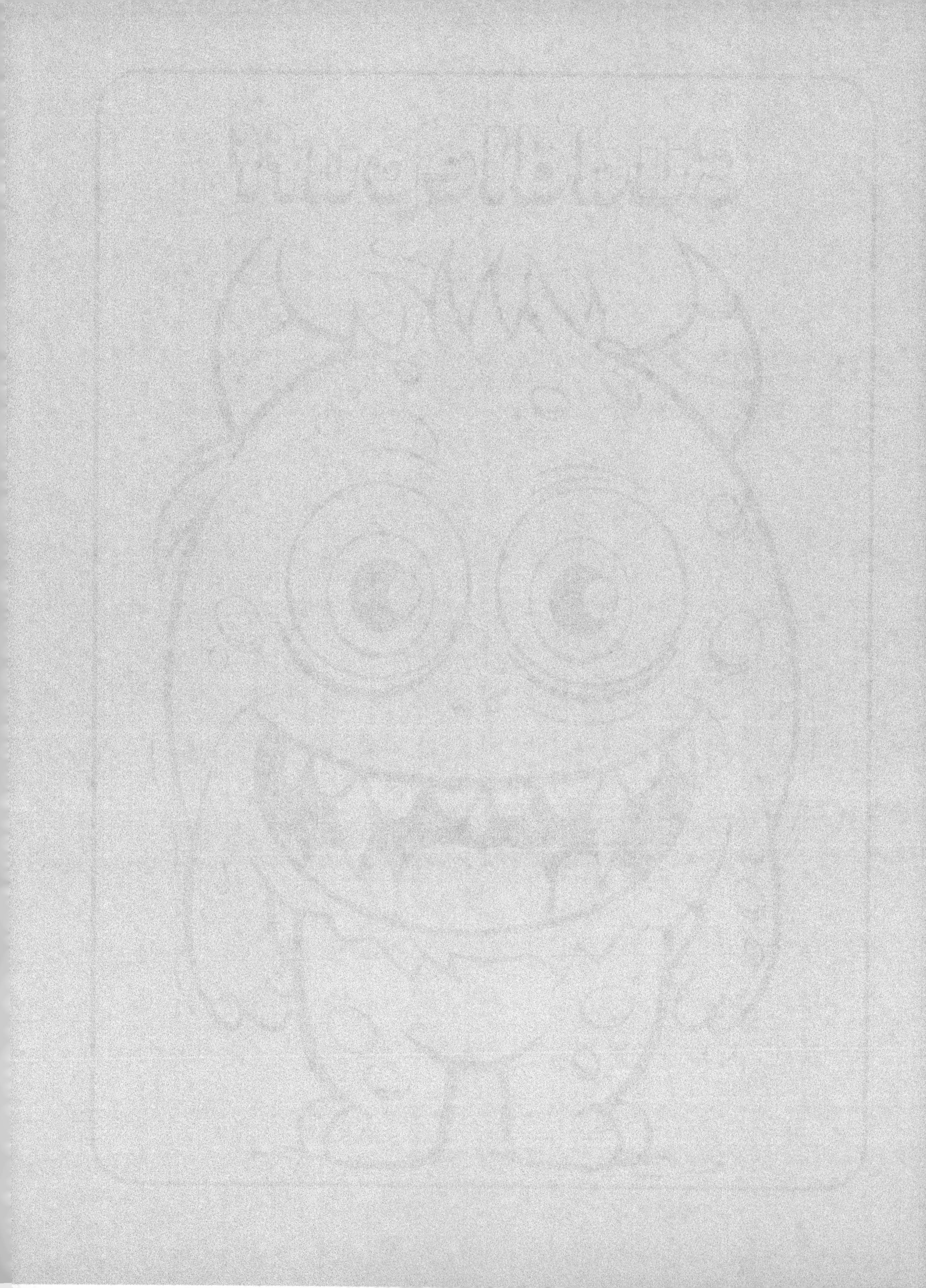

Sprinklewhisk

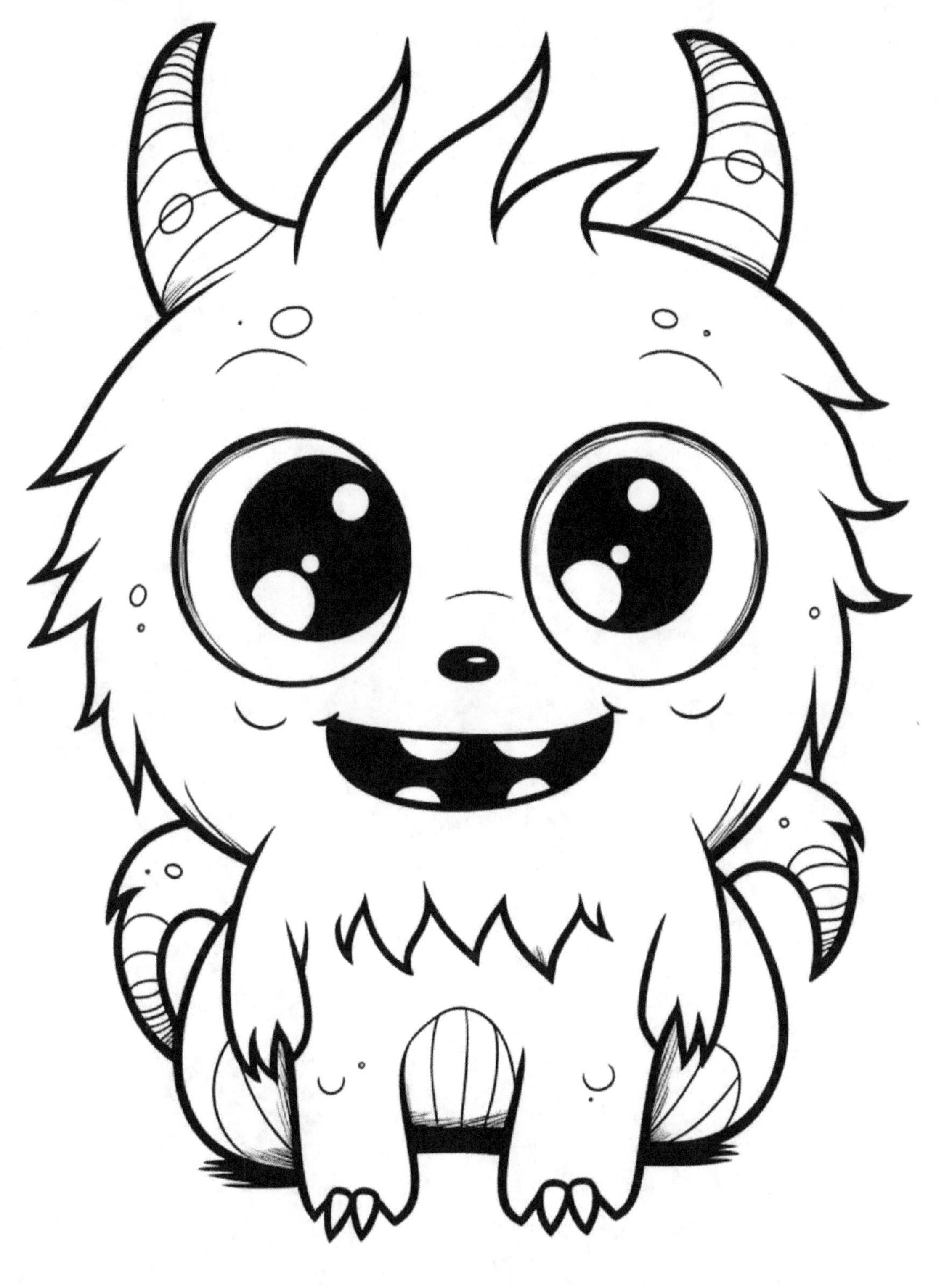

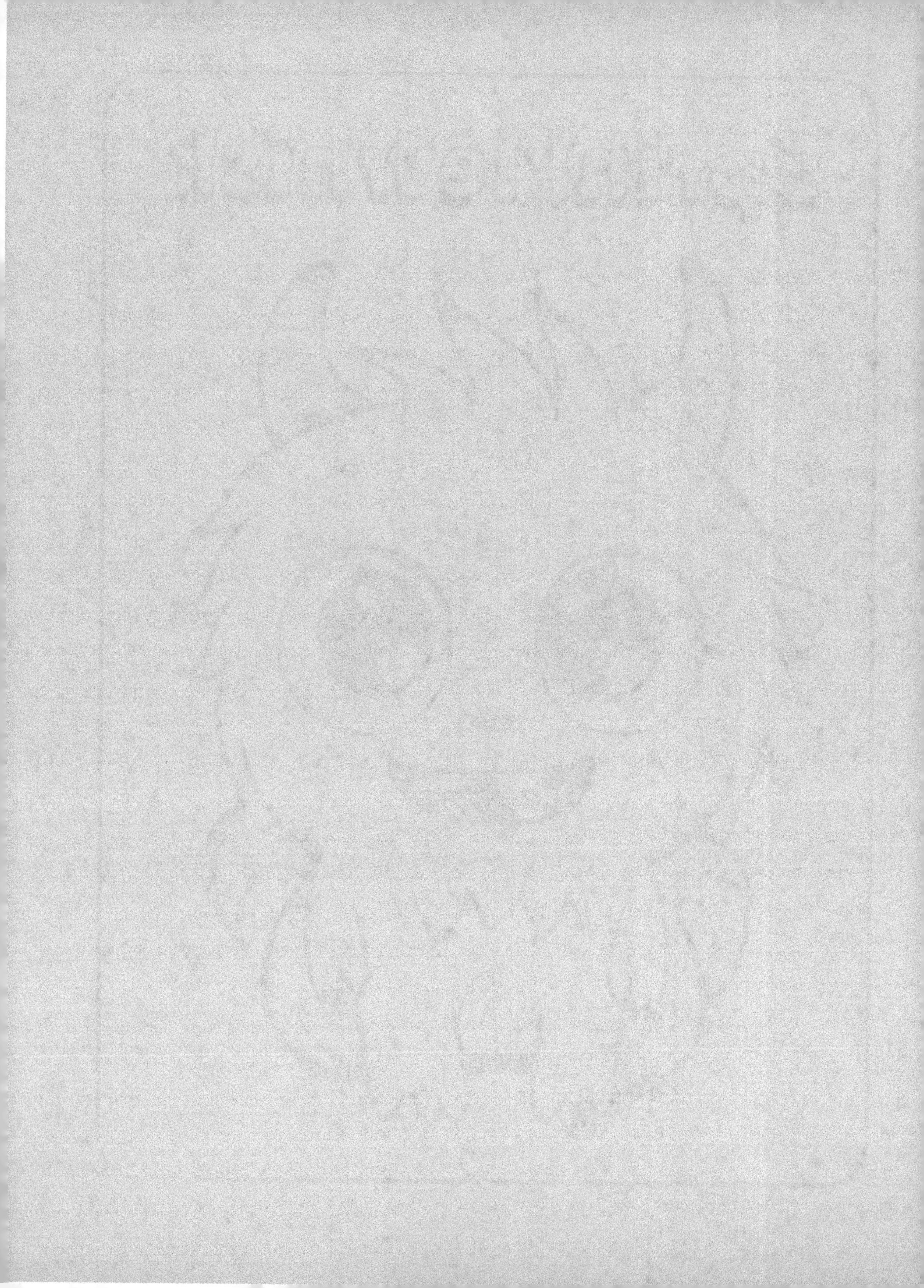

Snickerdoodle

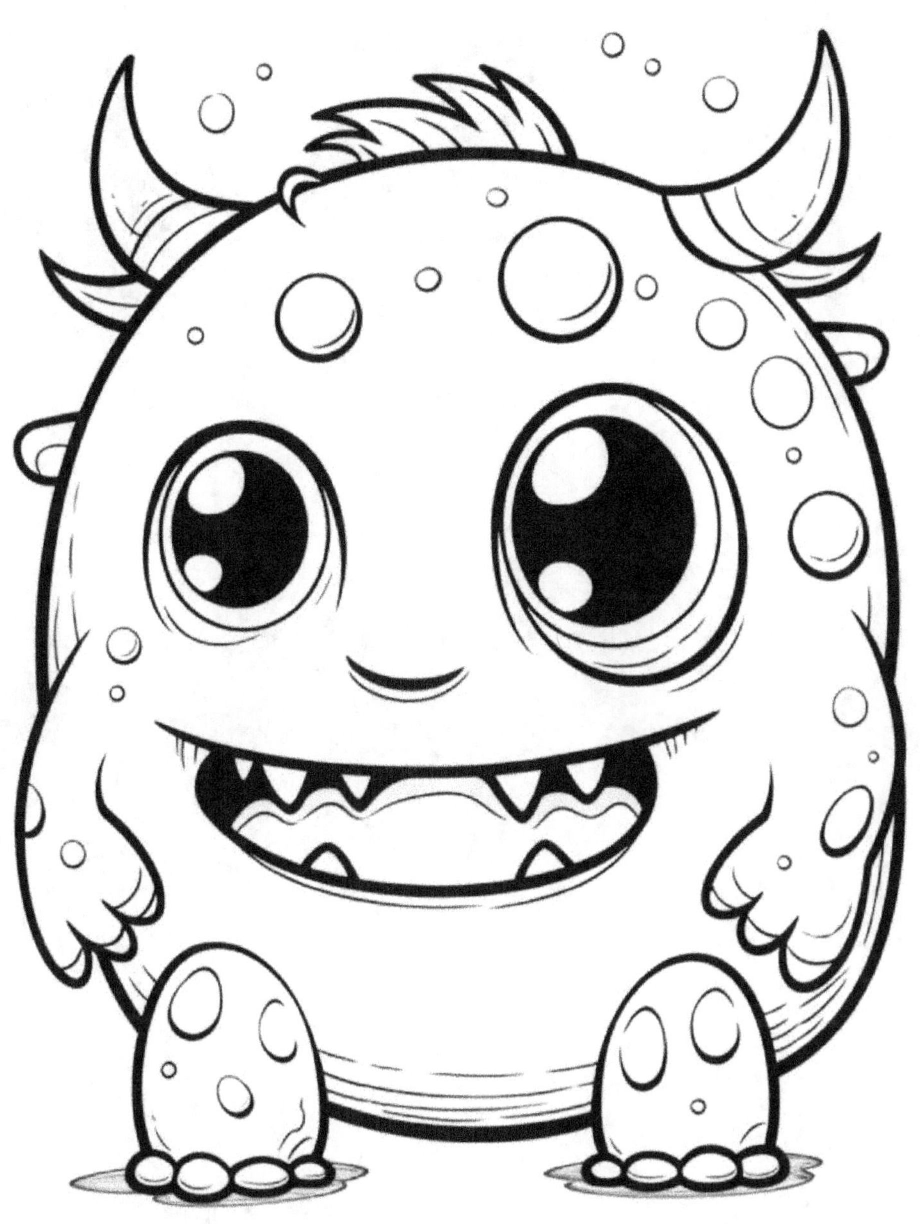

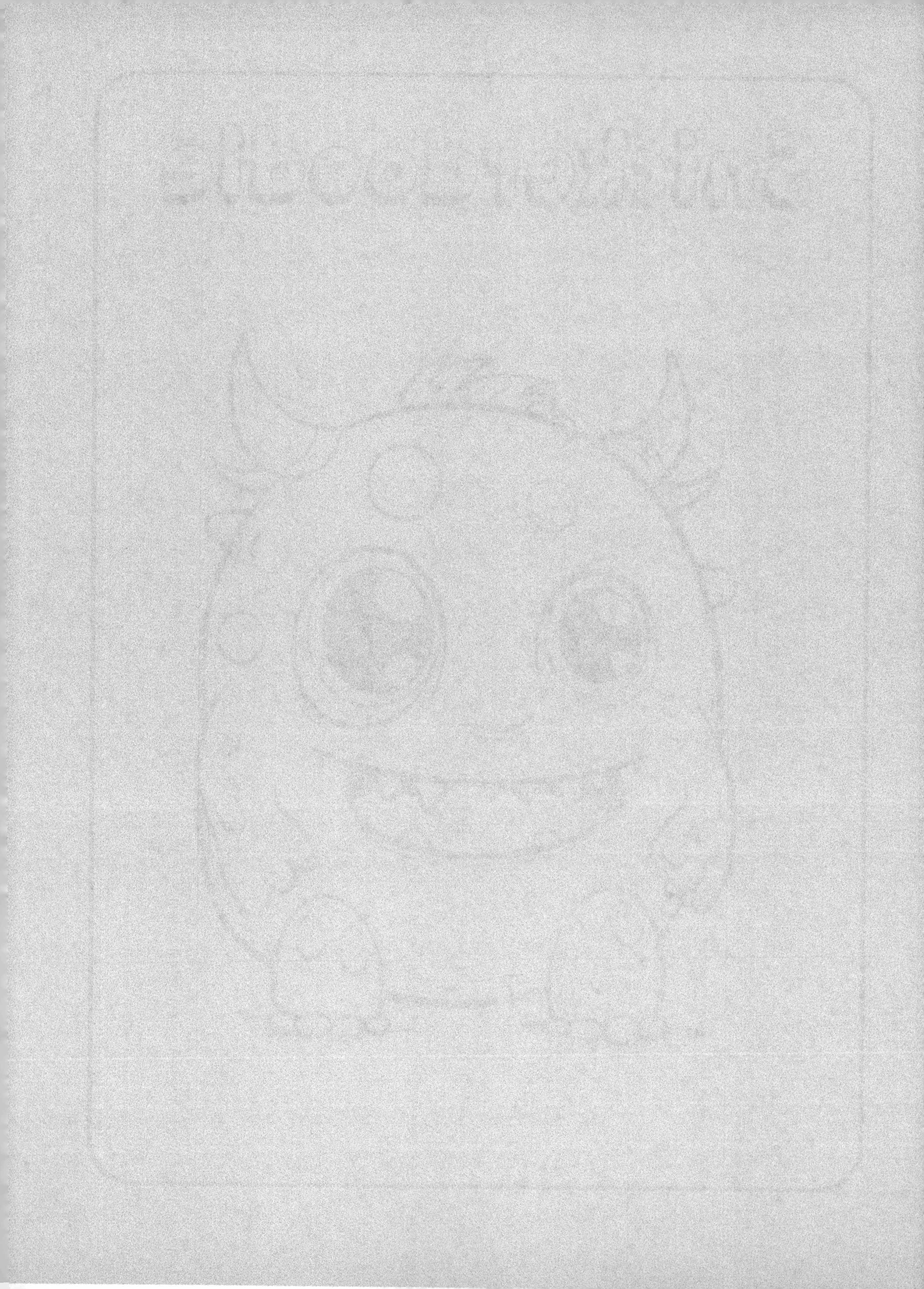

Squeakyfluff

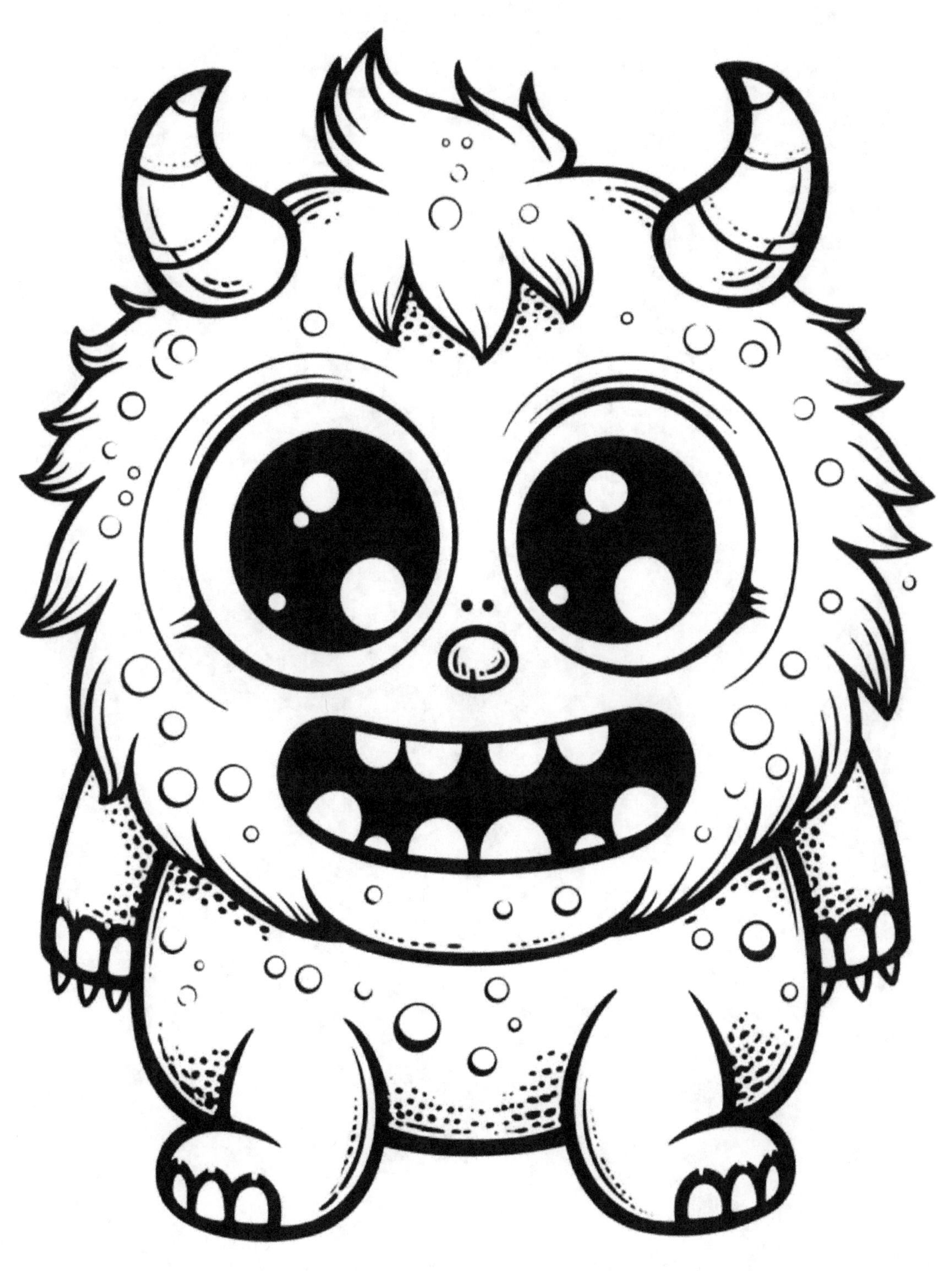

Twinklebump

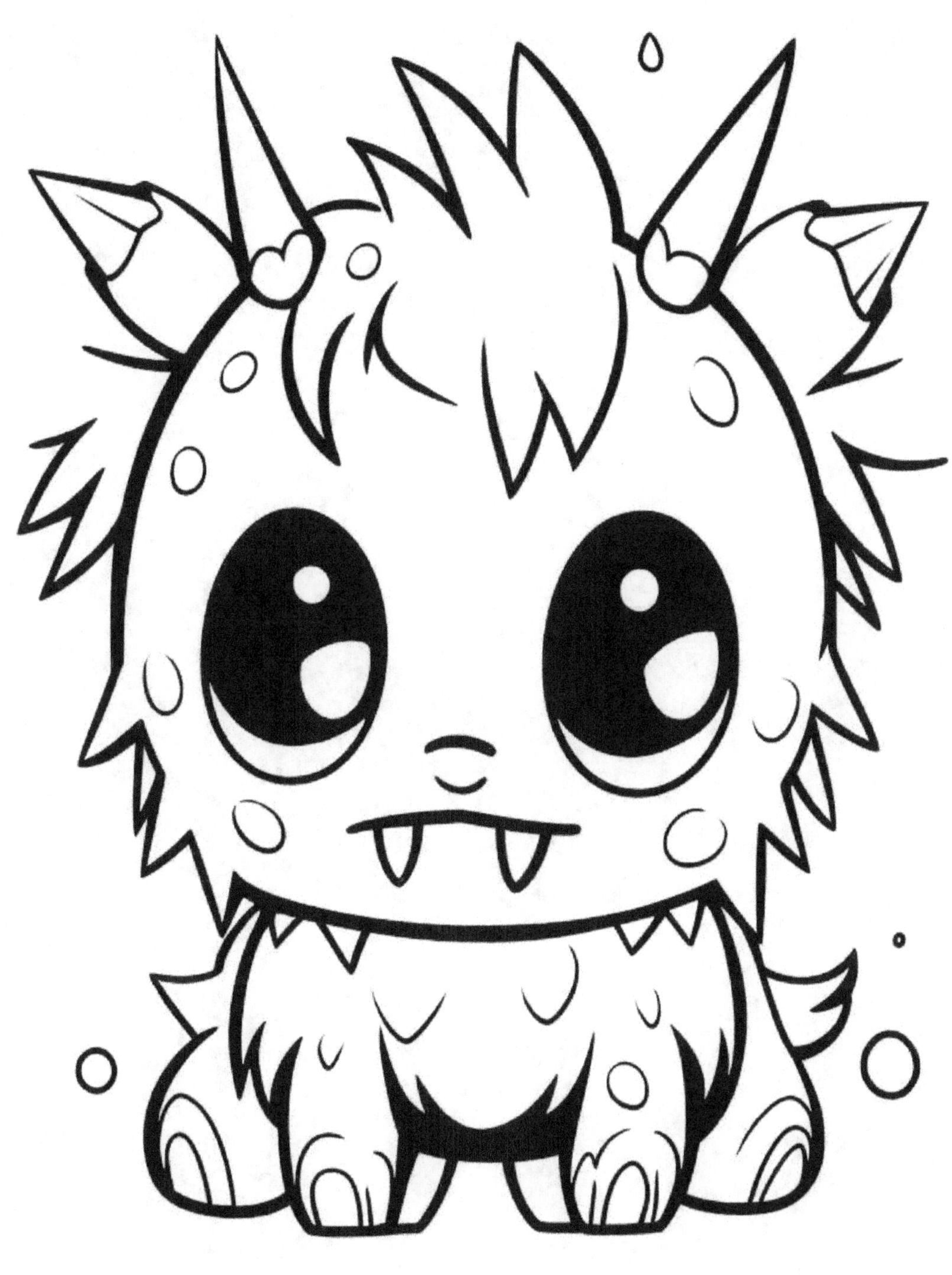

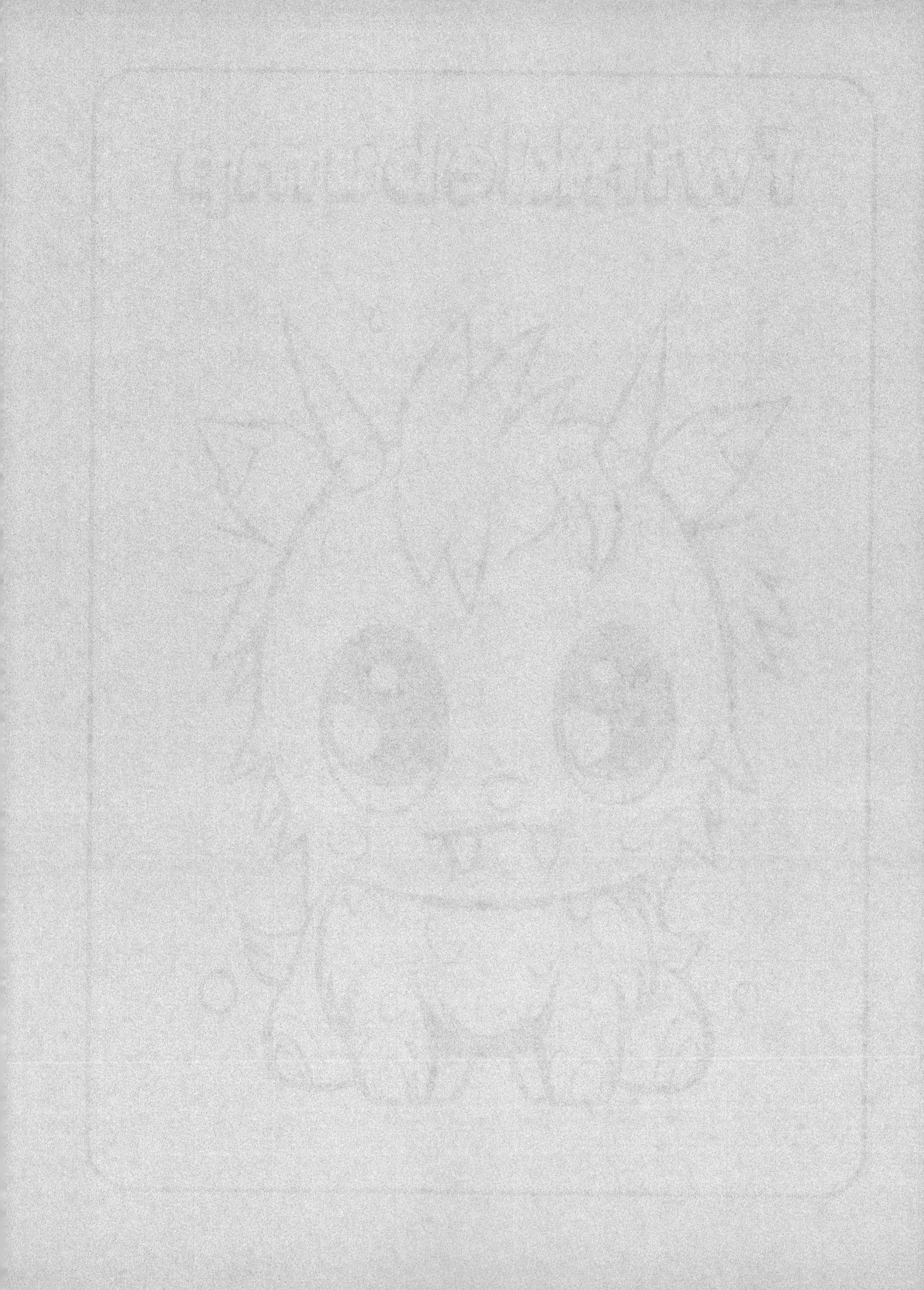

Puddlejump

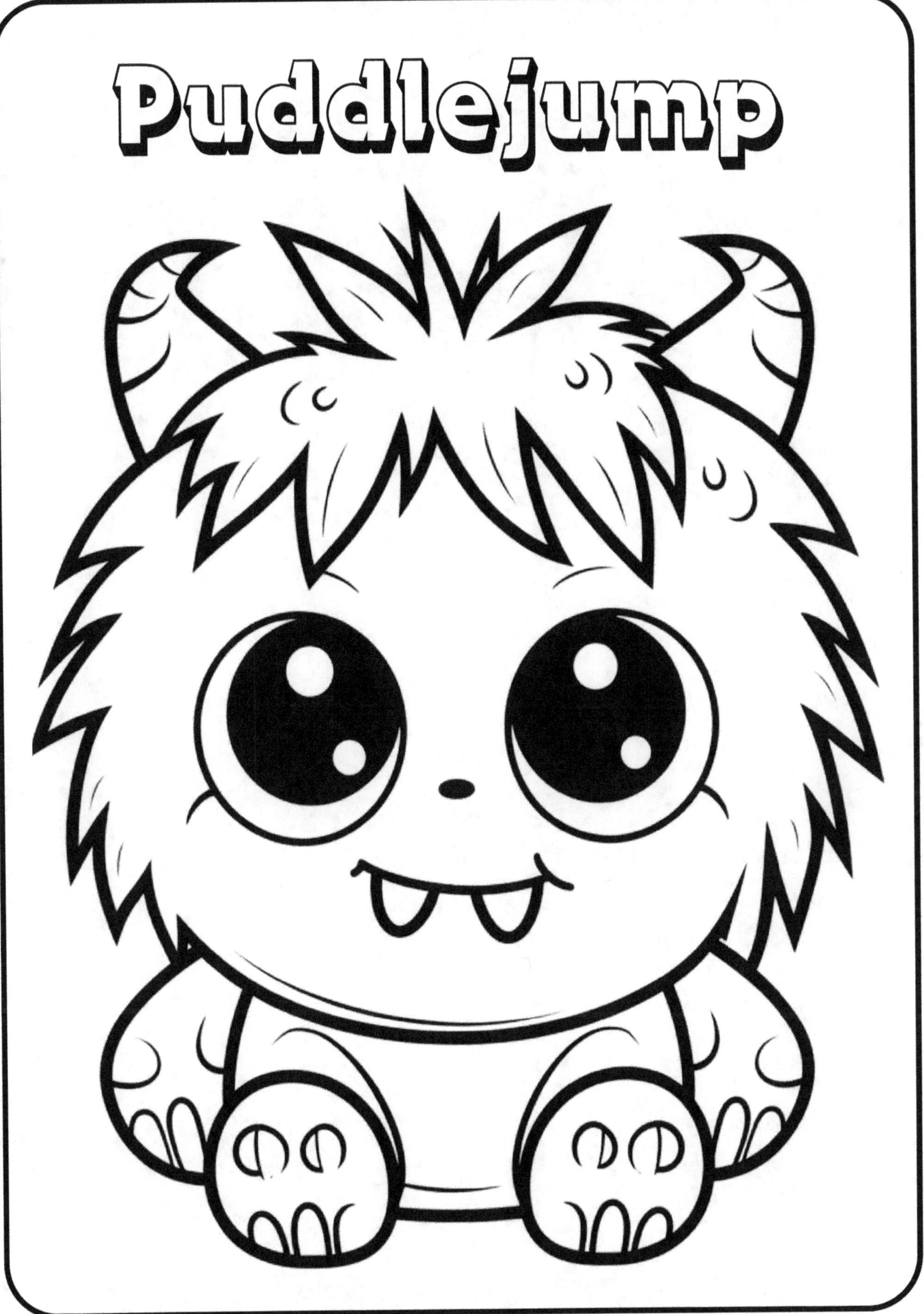

Wigglywump

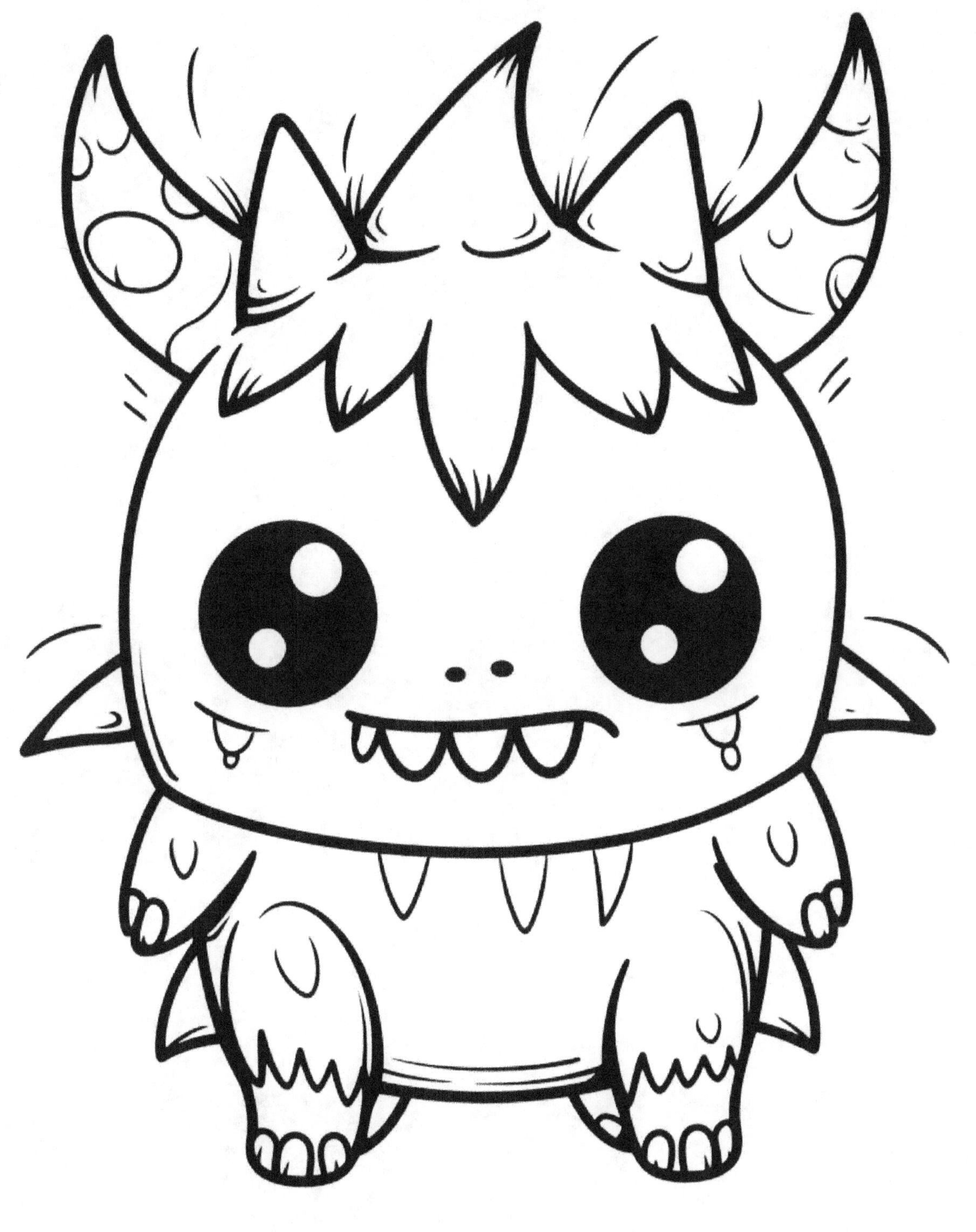

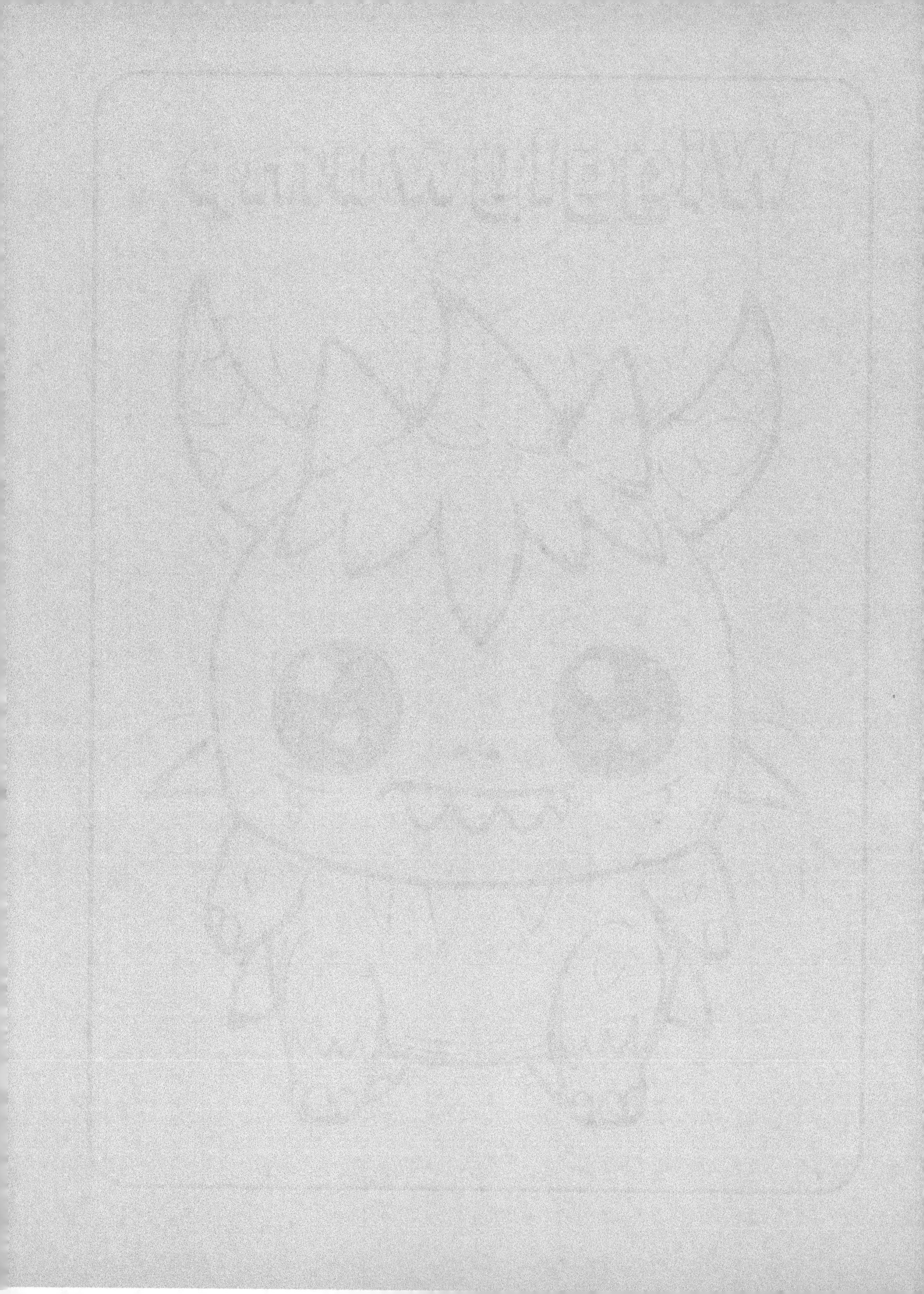

Snickerdoodle

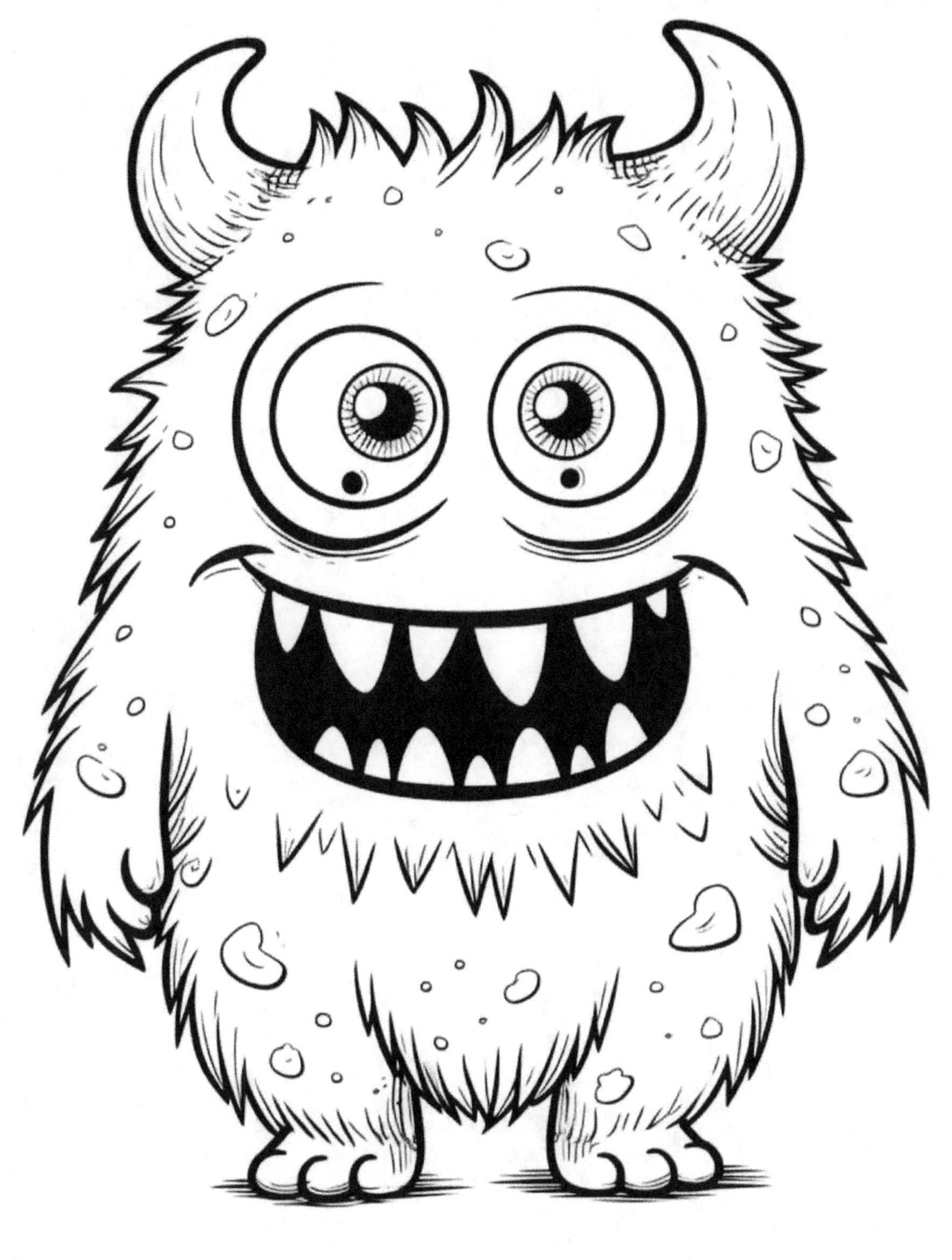

Jollygiggle

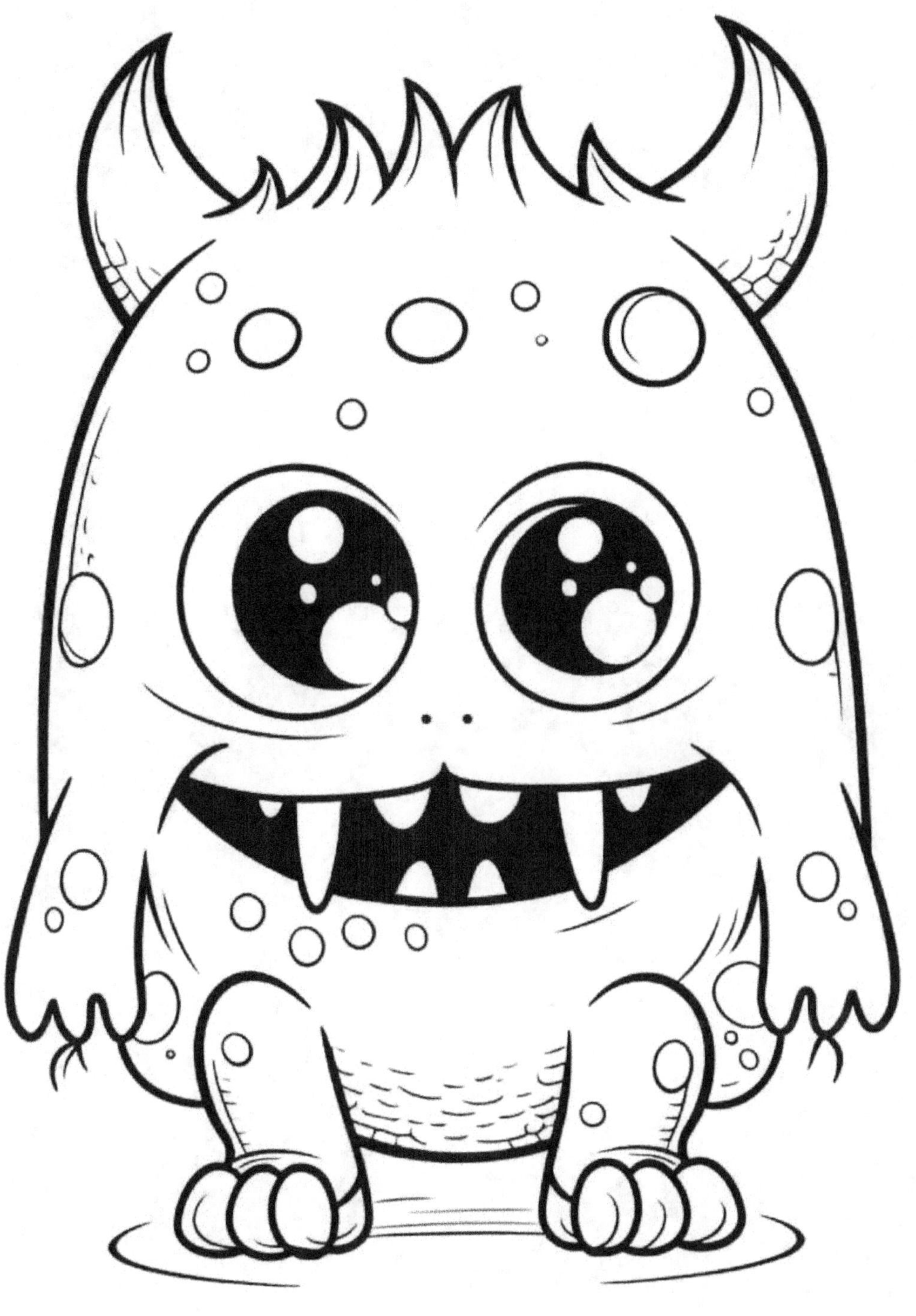

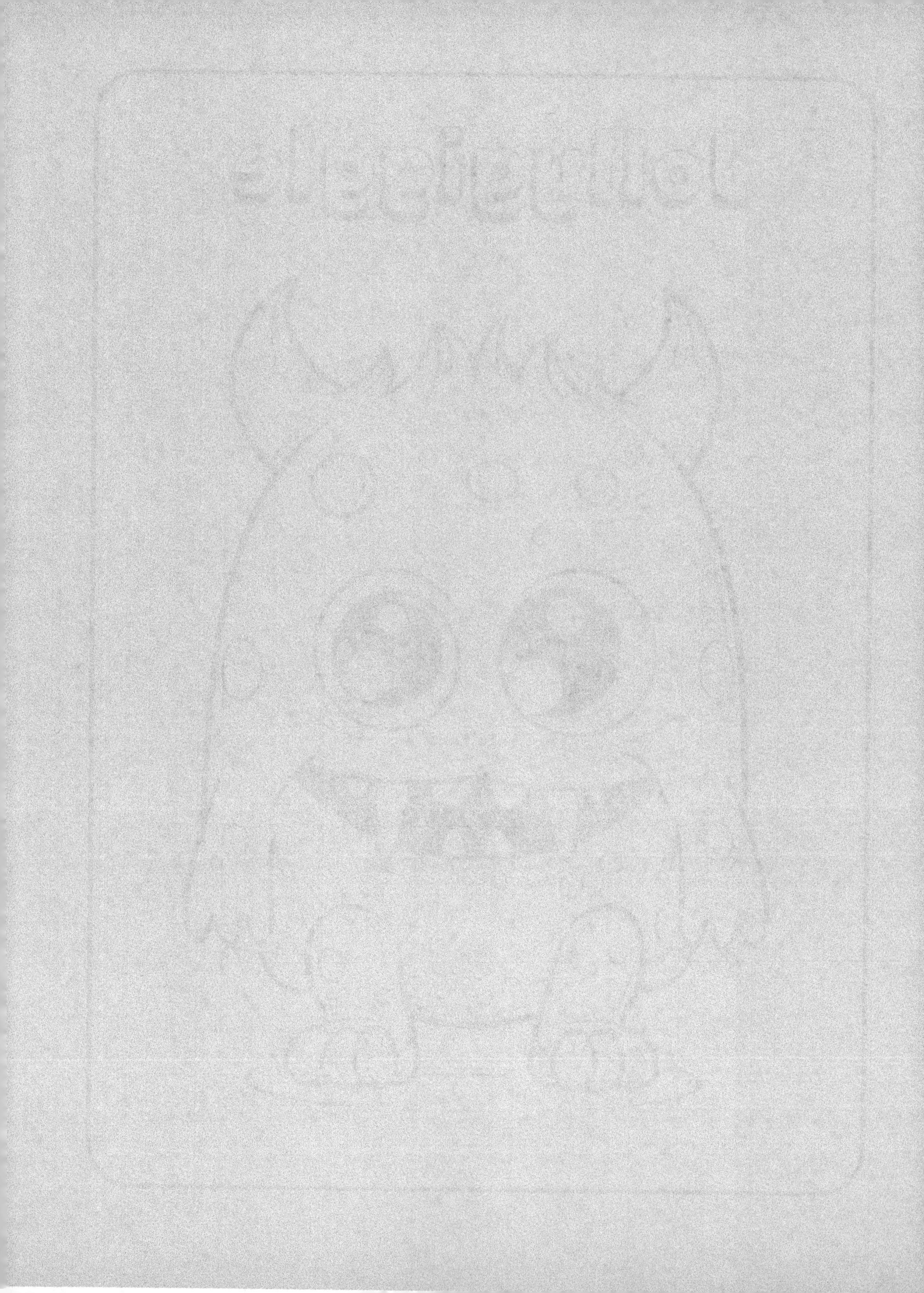

Fuzzysnuggle

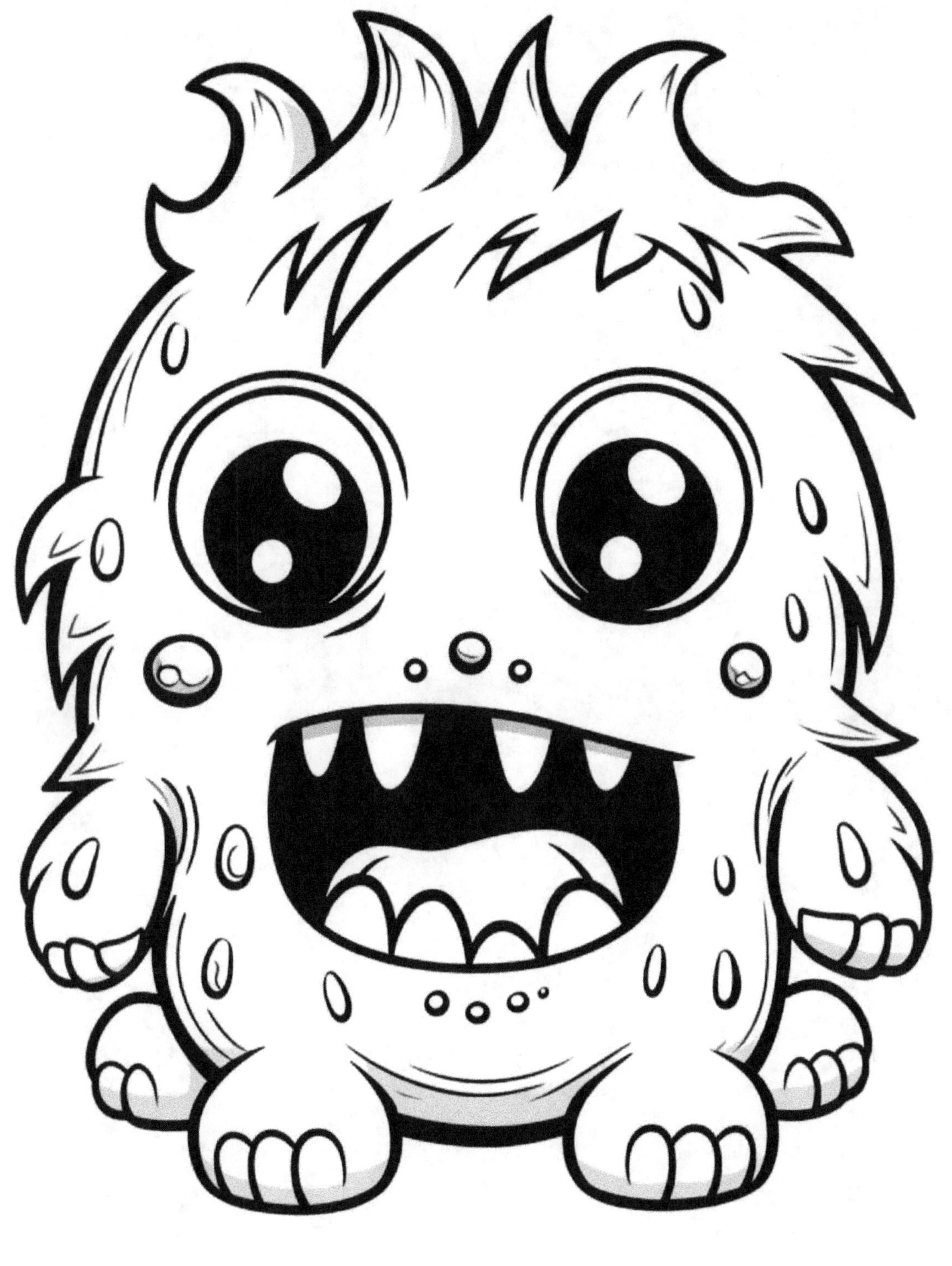

Dandydoodle

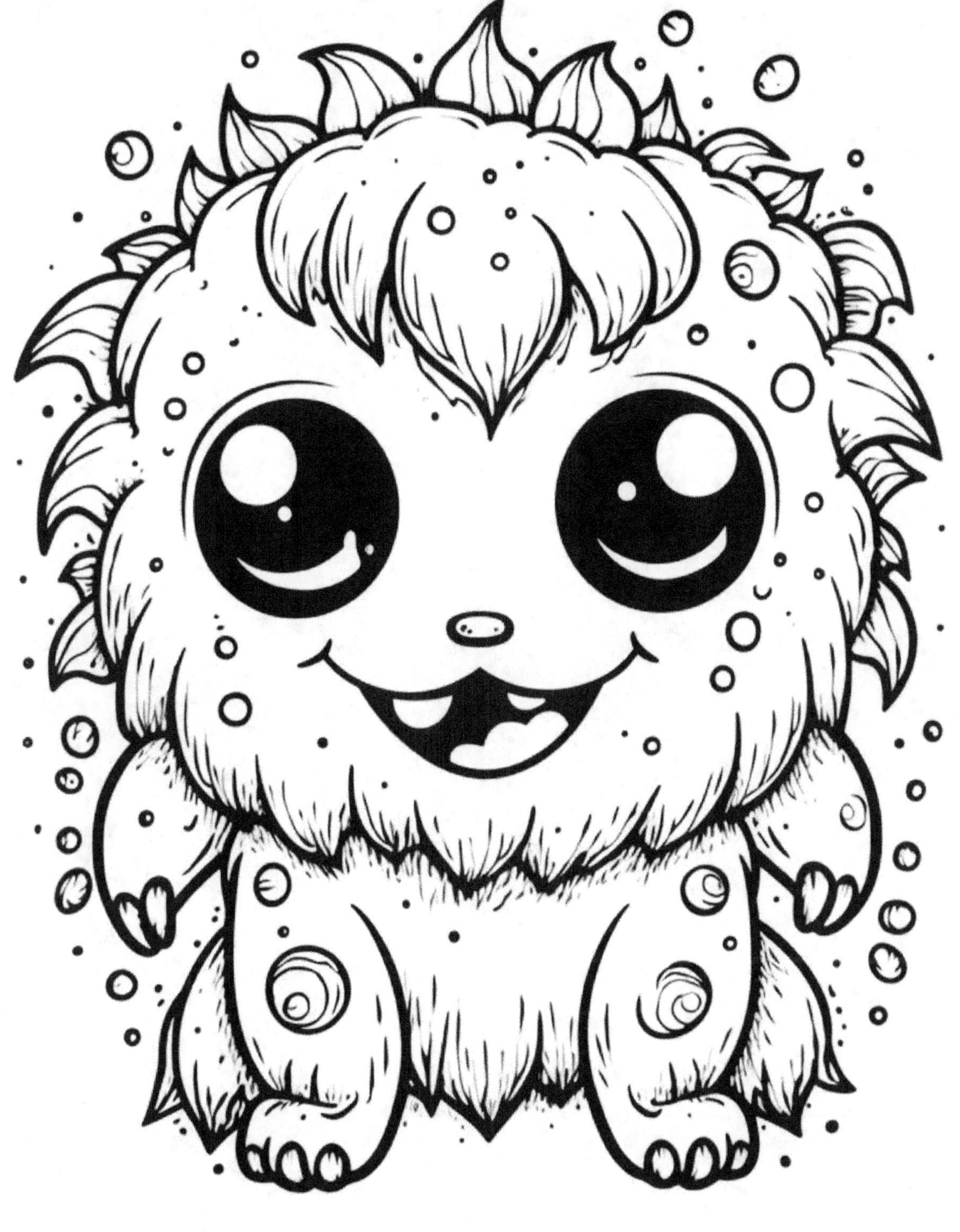

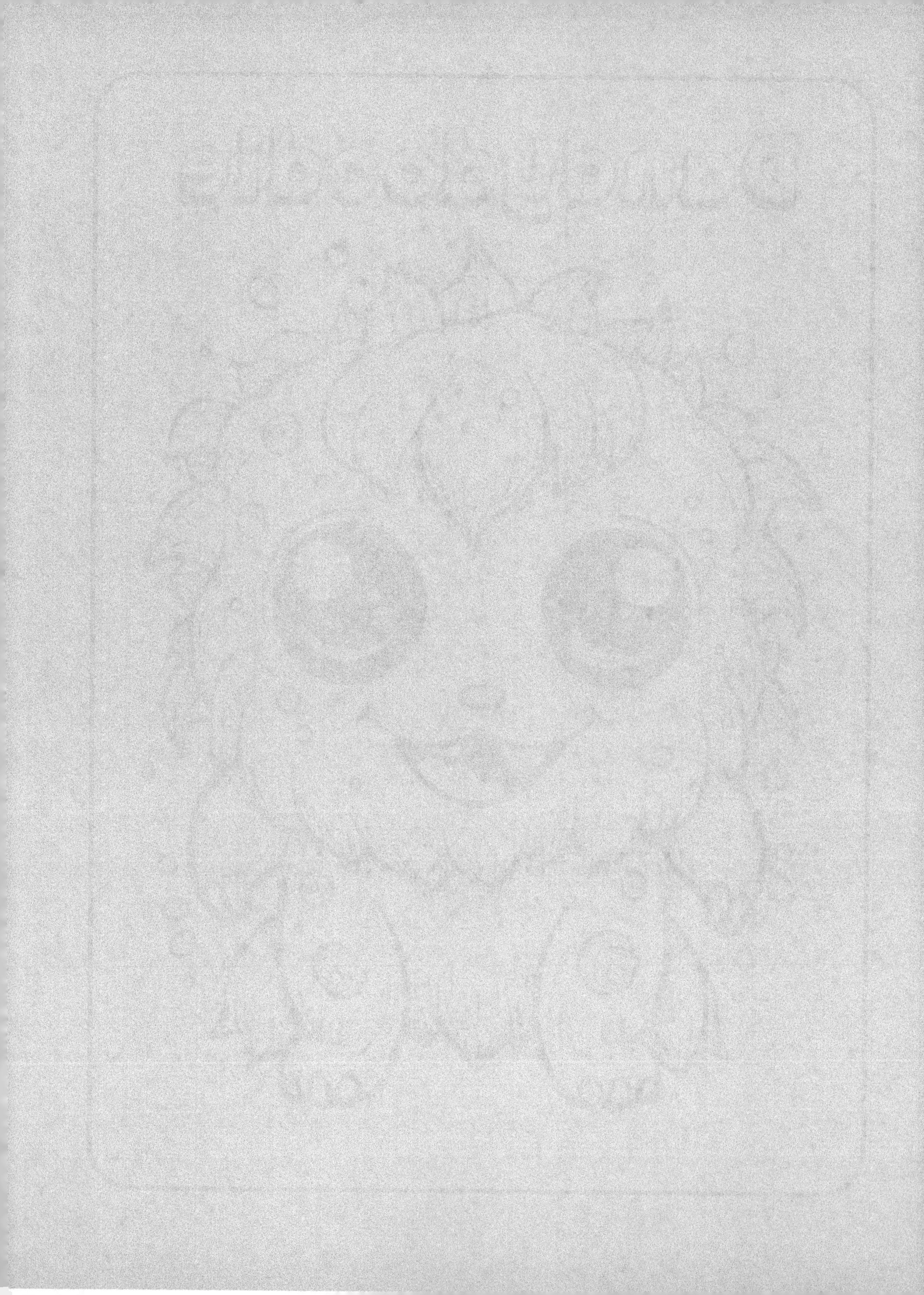

Bumblebop

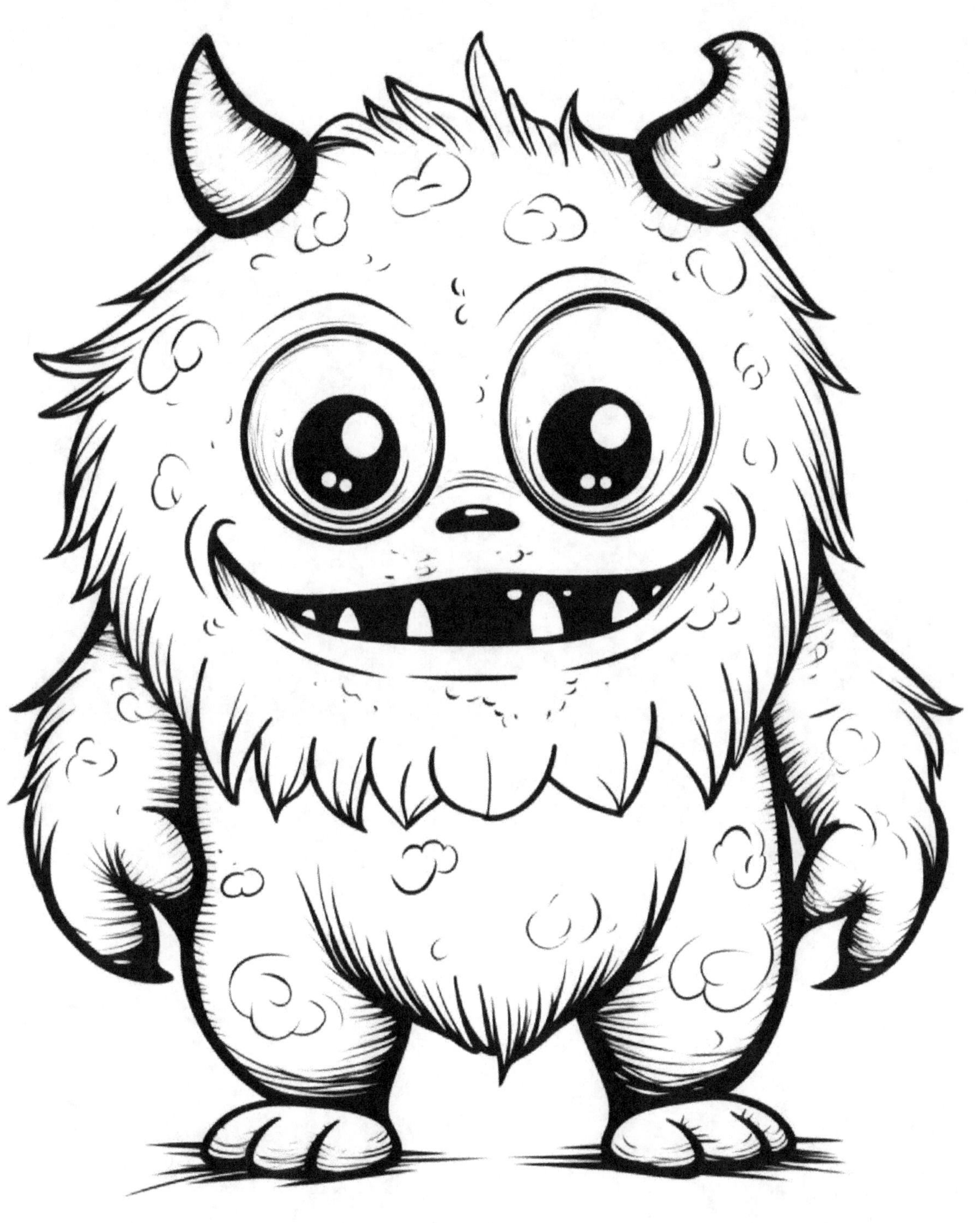

Furrywhisk

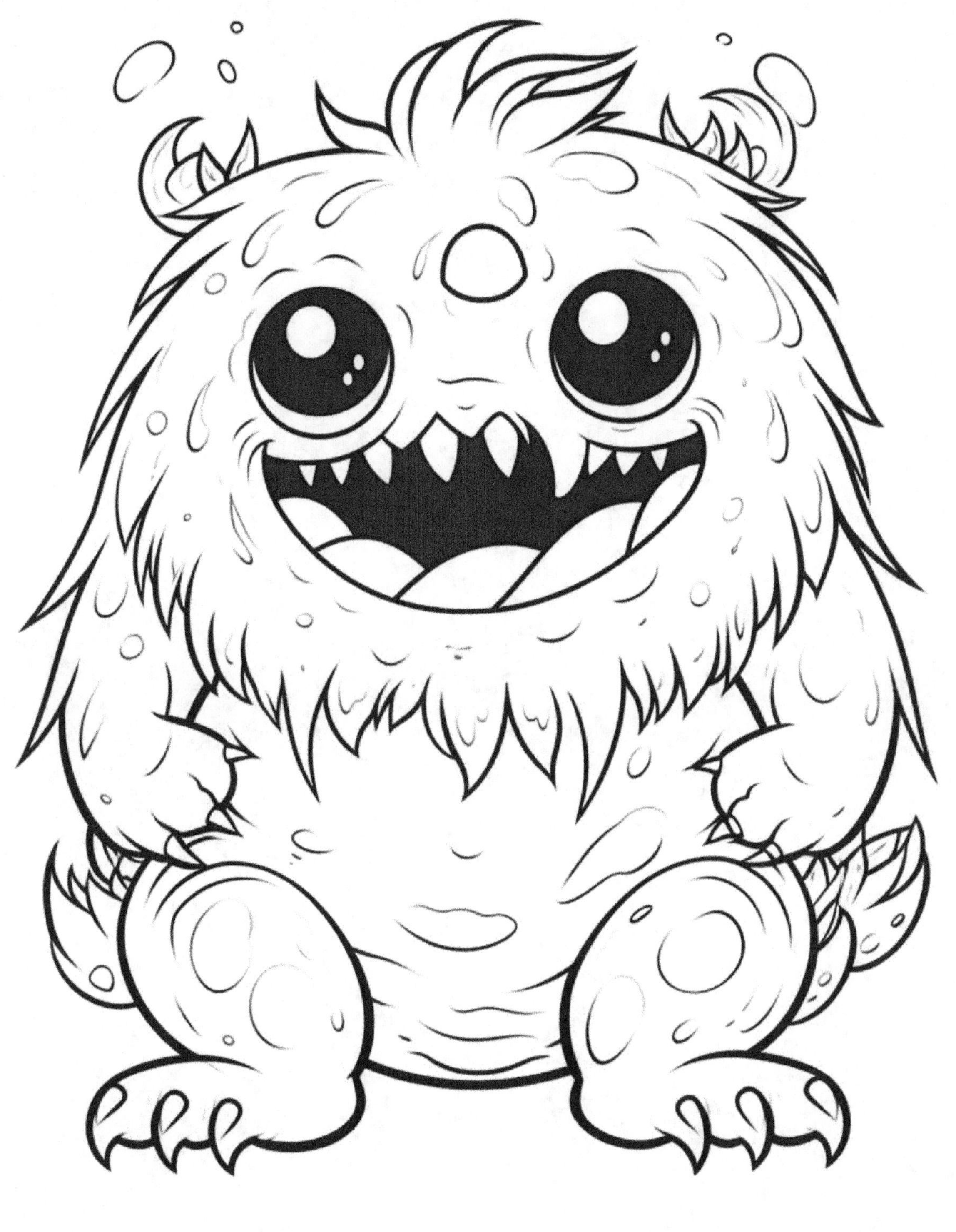

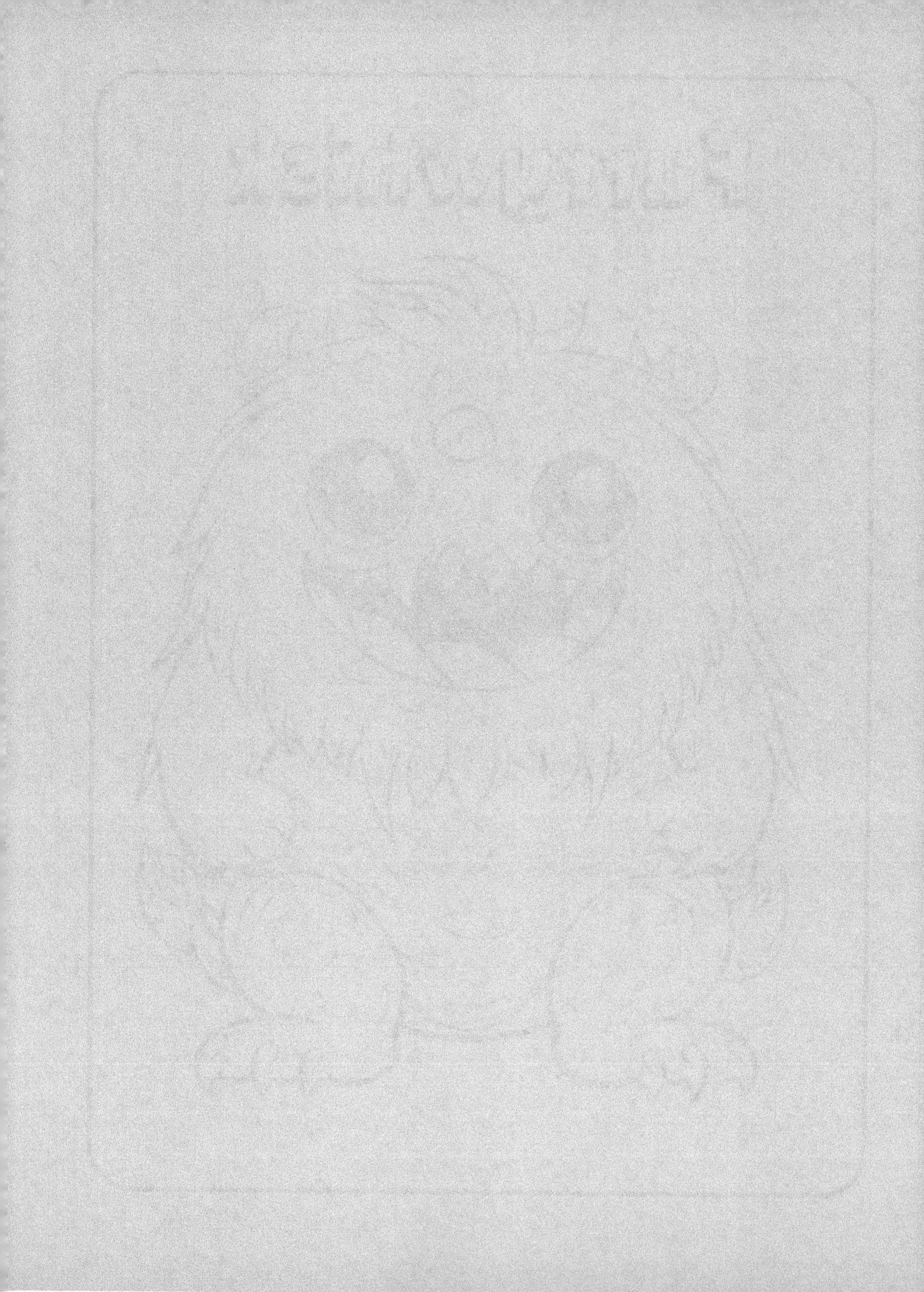

Snickerdoo

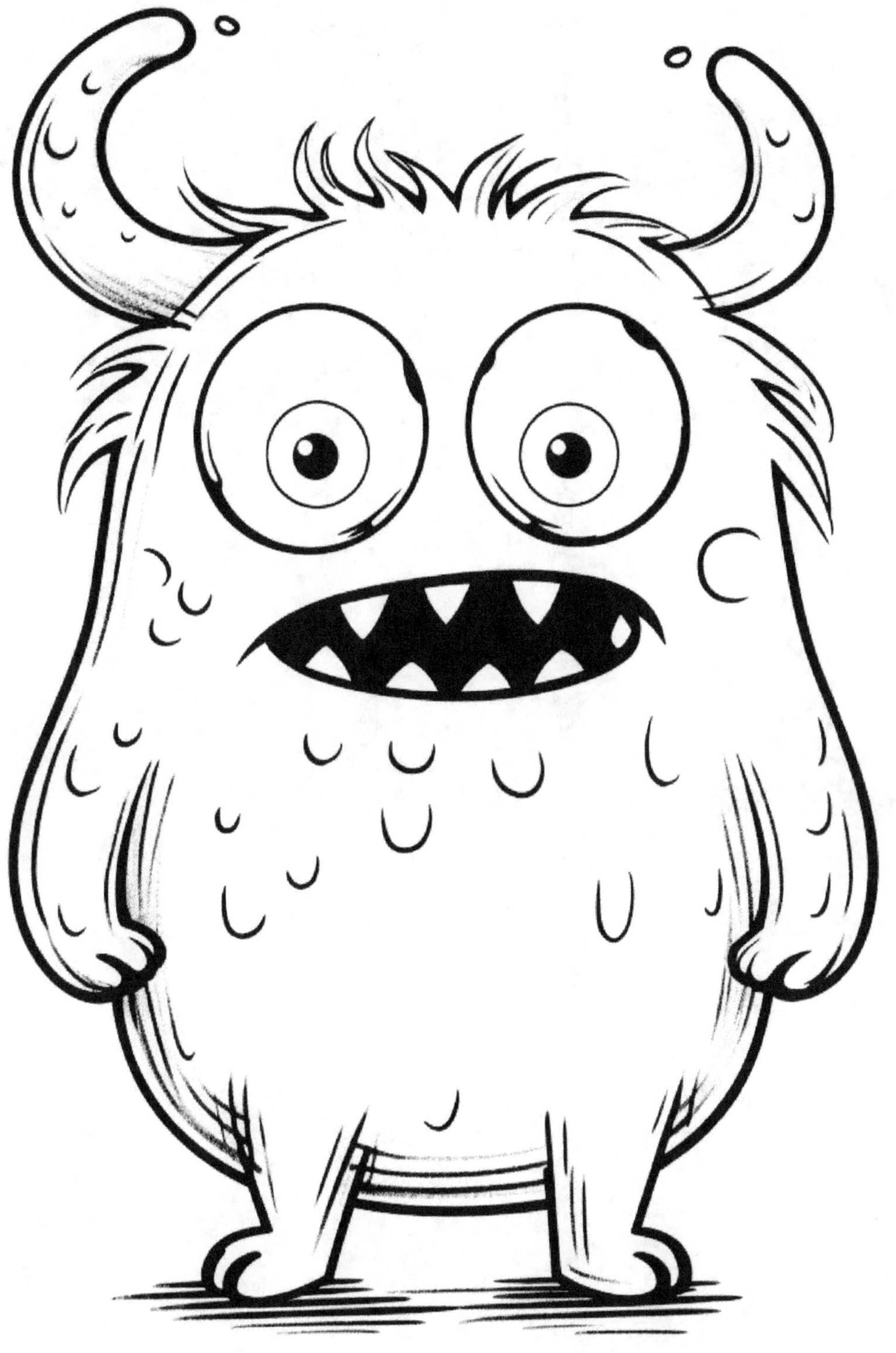

Ticklepuff

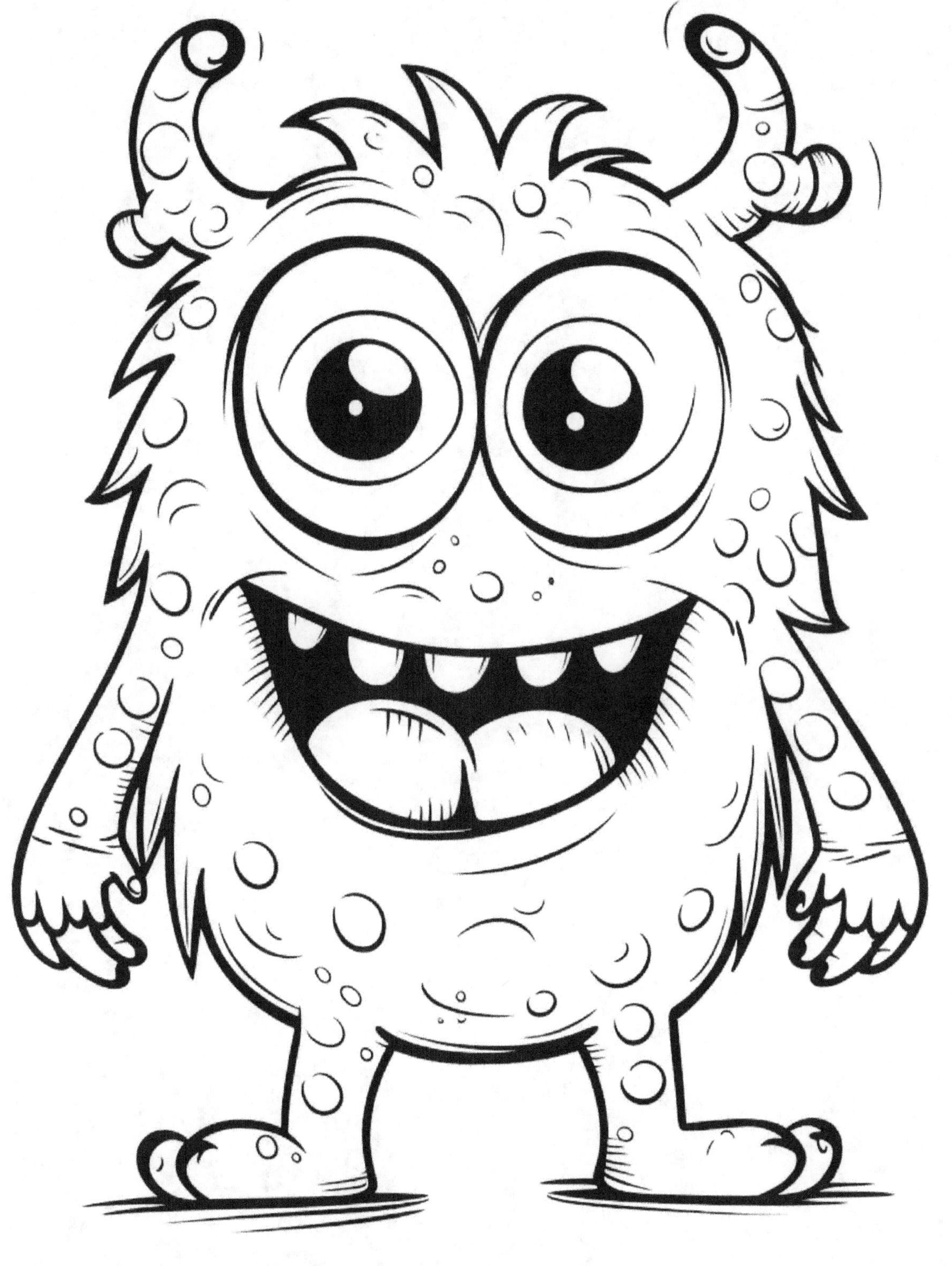

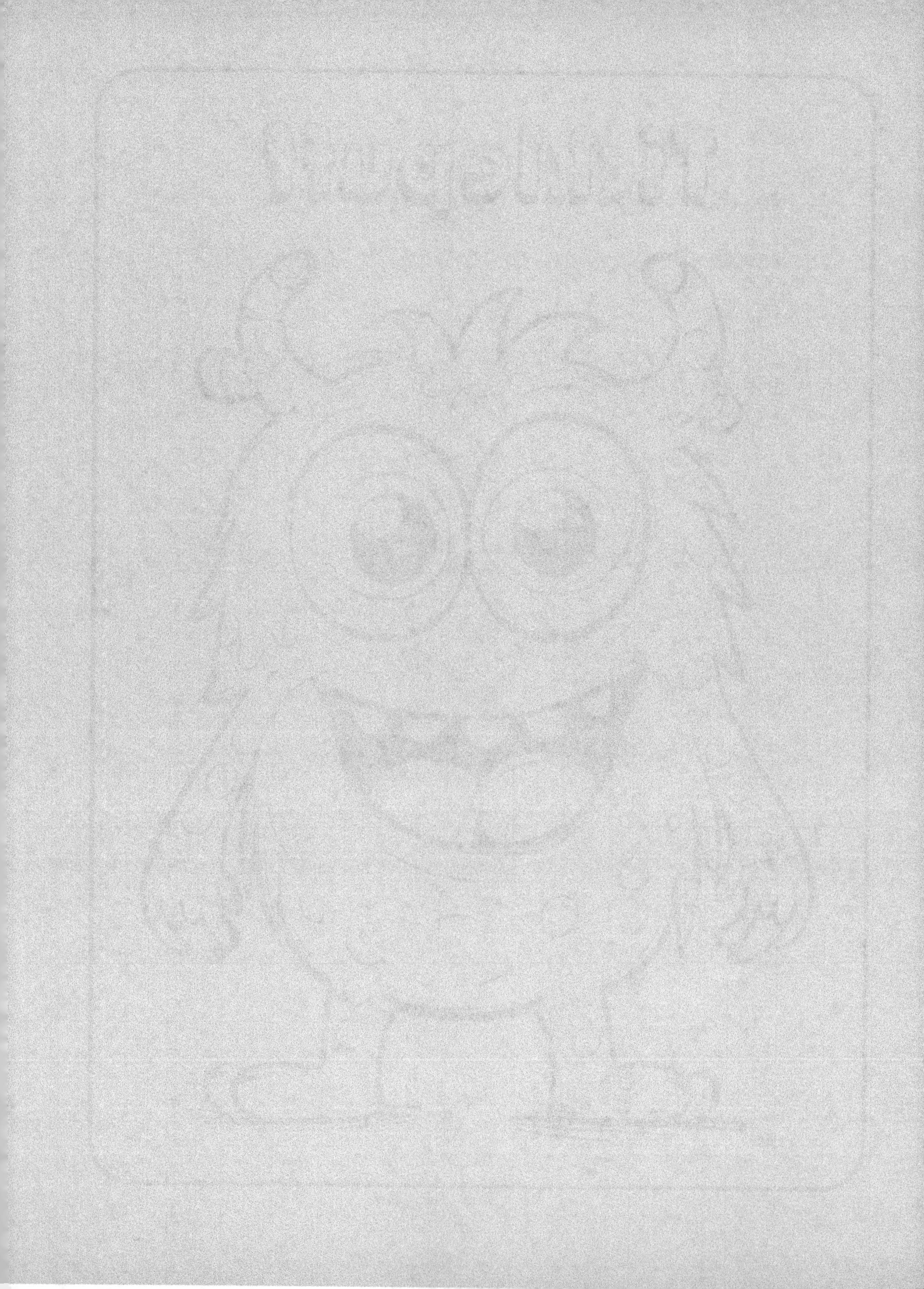

Dizzytwirl

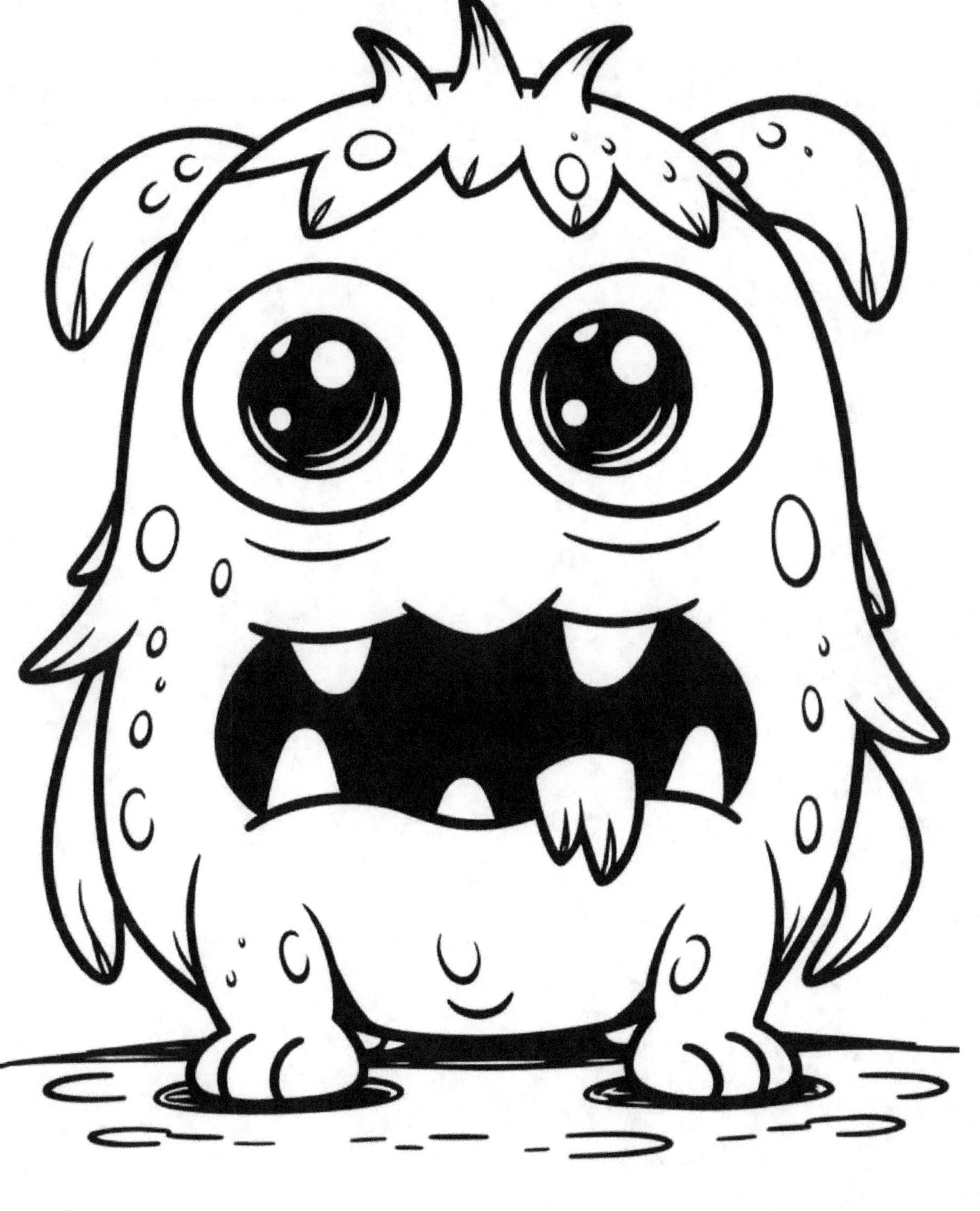

Glimmergig

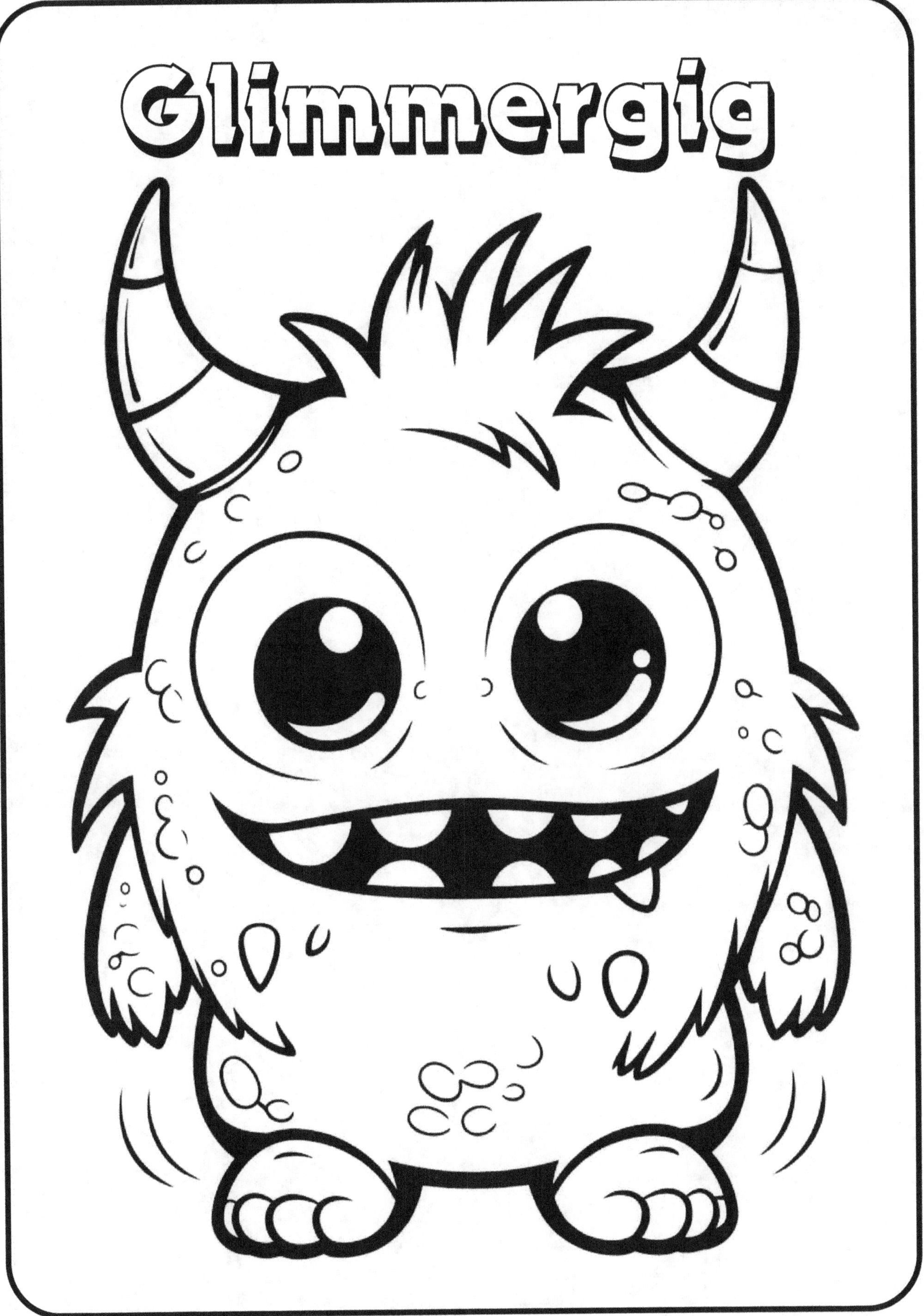

Jellybean

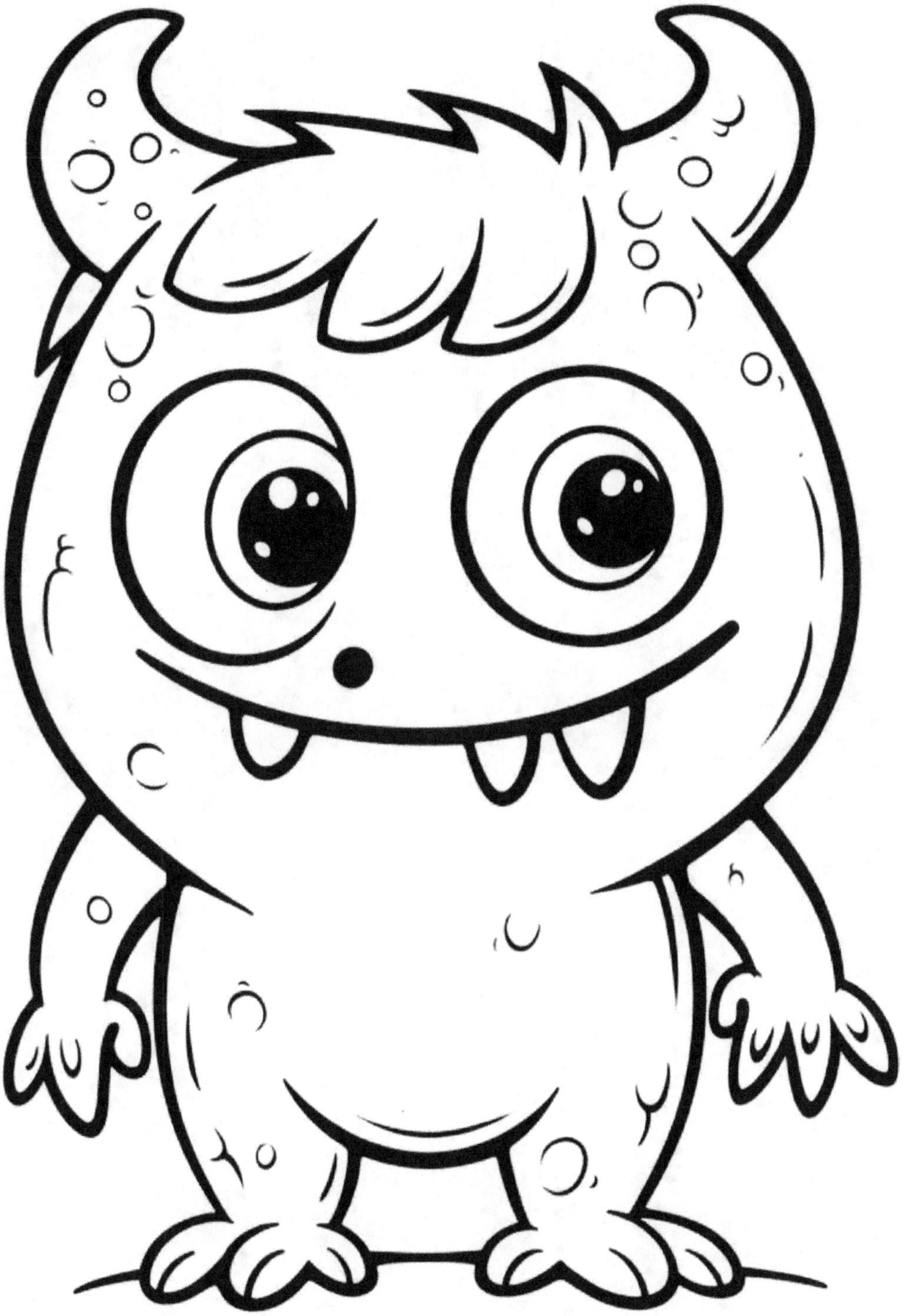

Gigglyglop

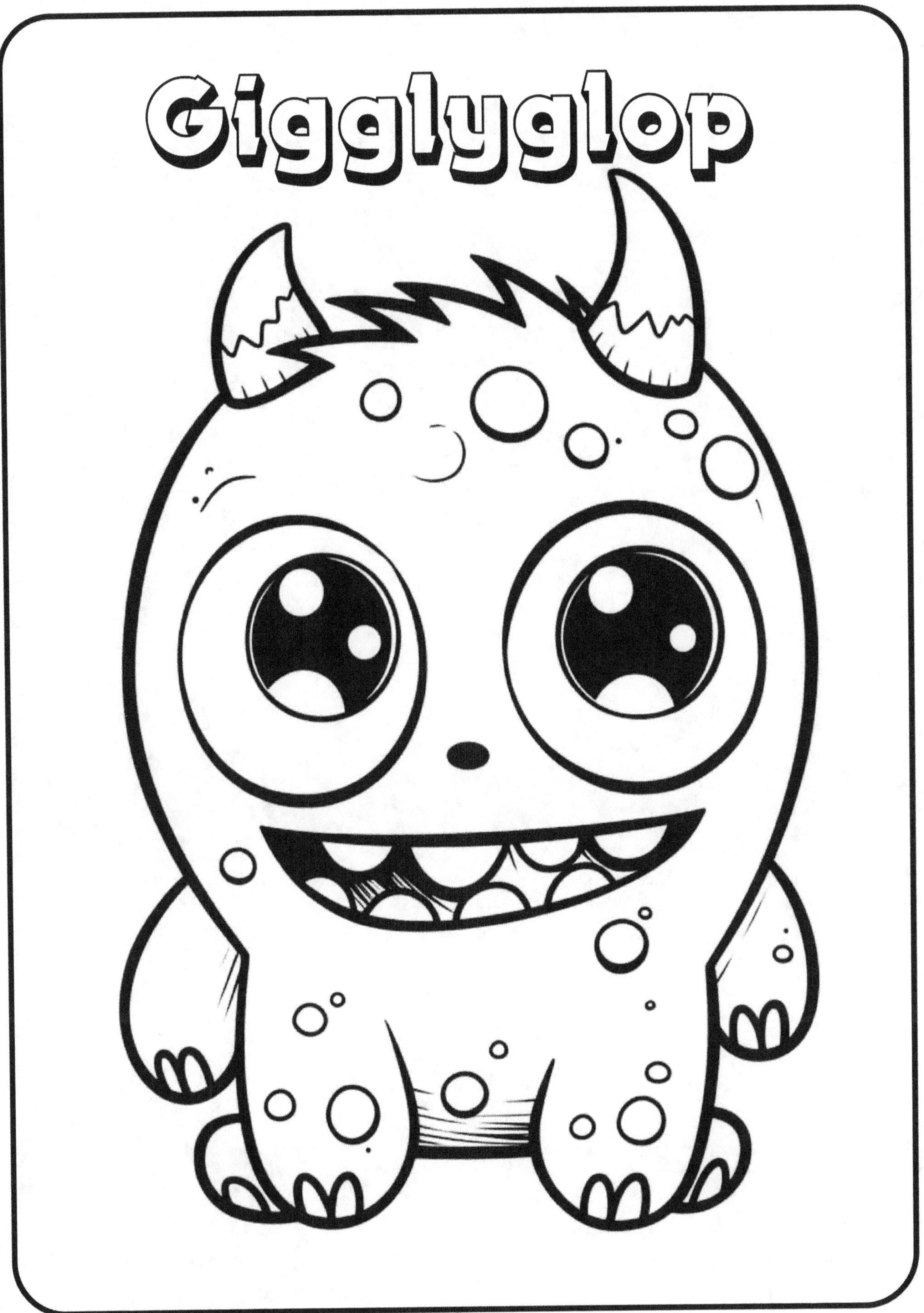

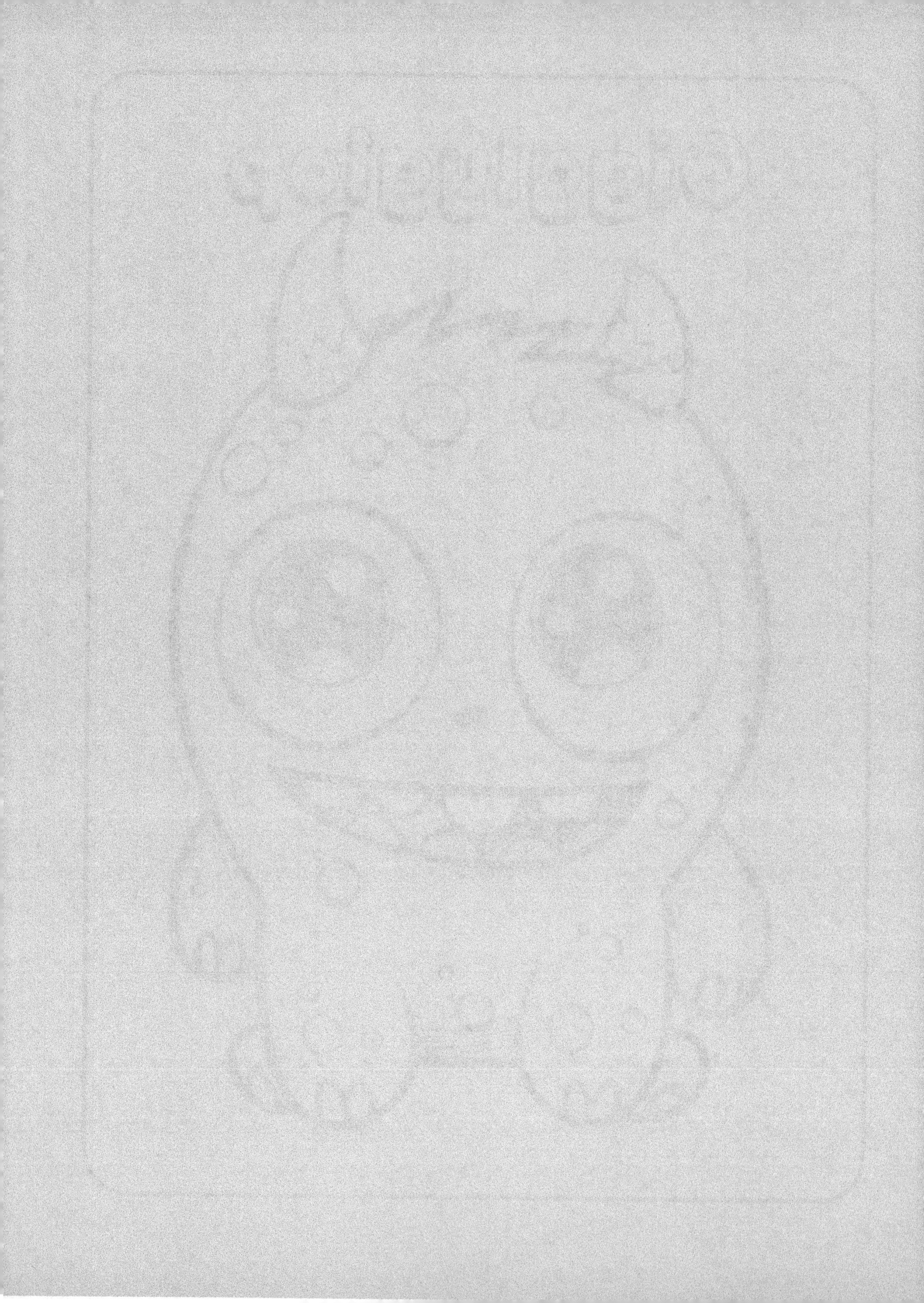

Whiskerwobble

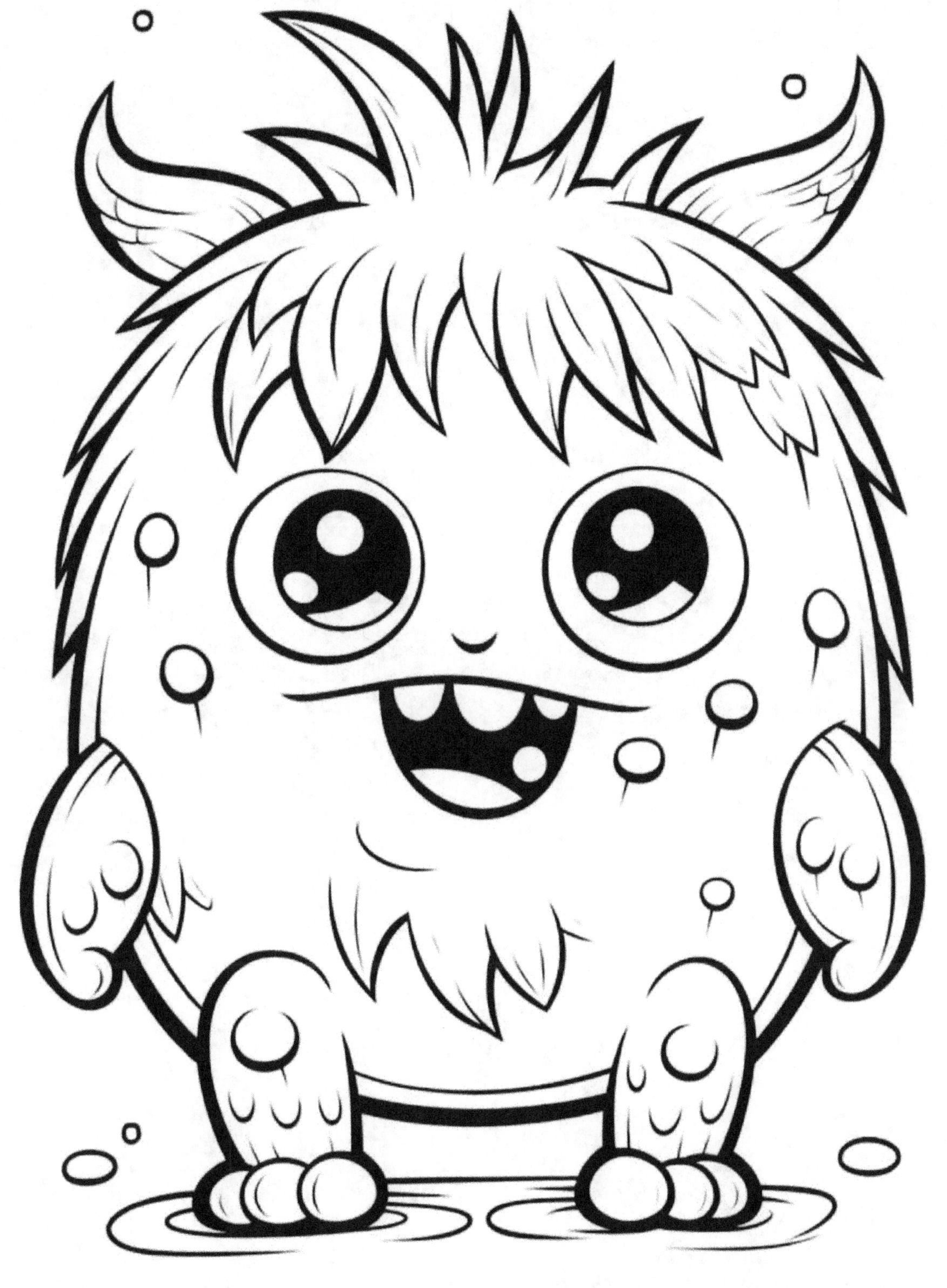

Snugglefuzz

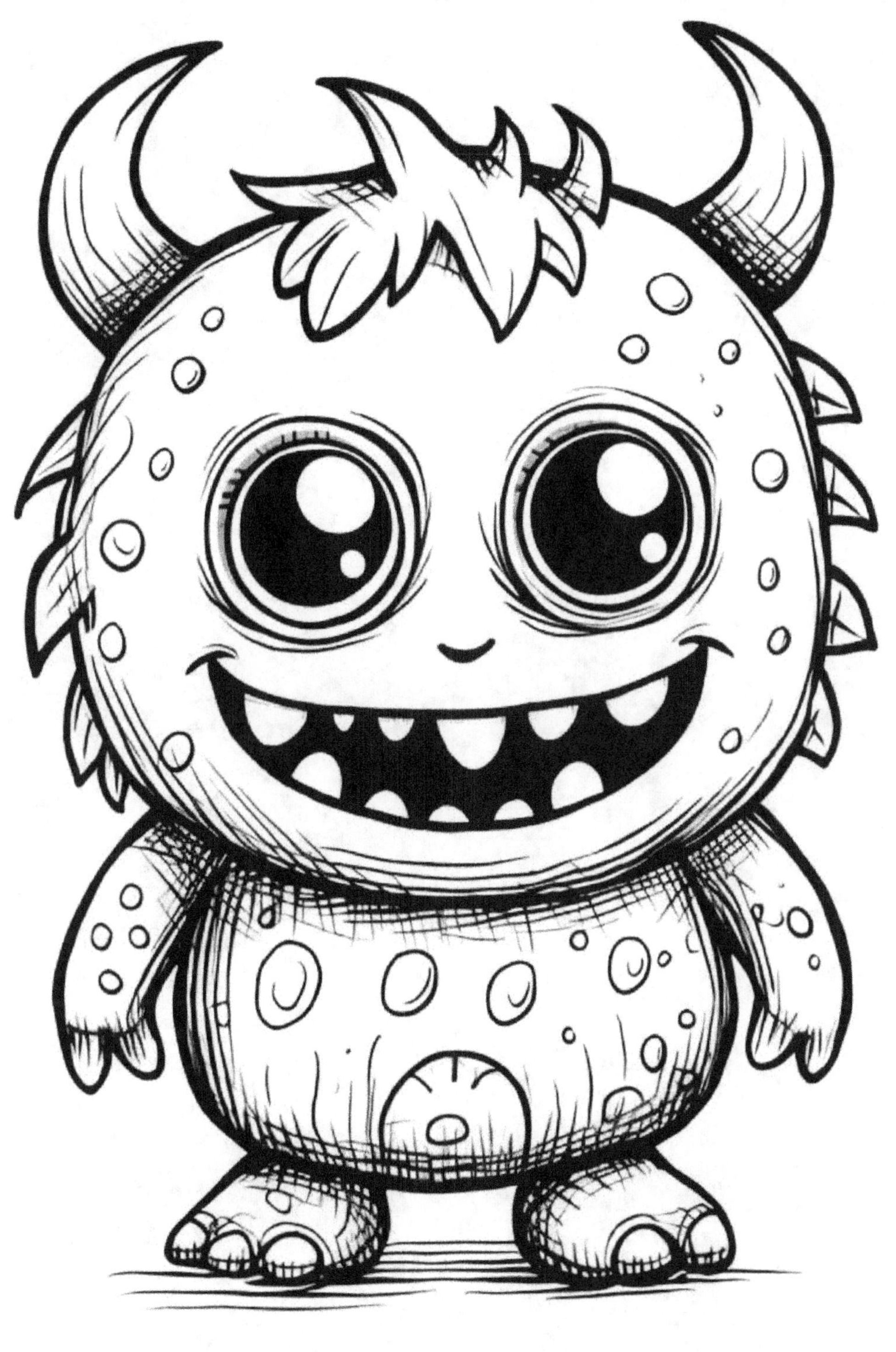

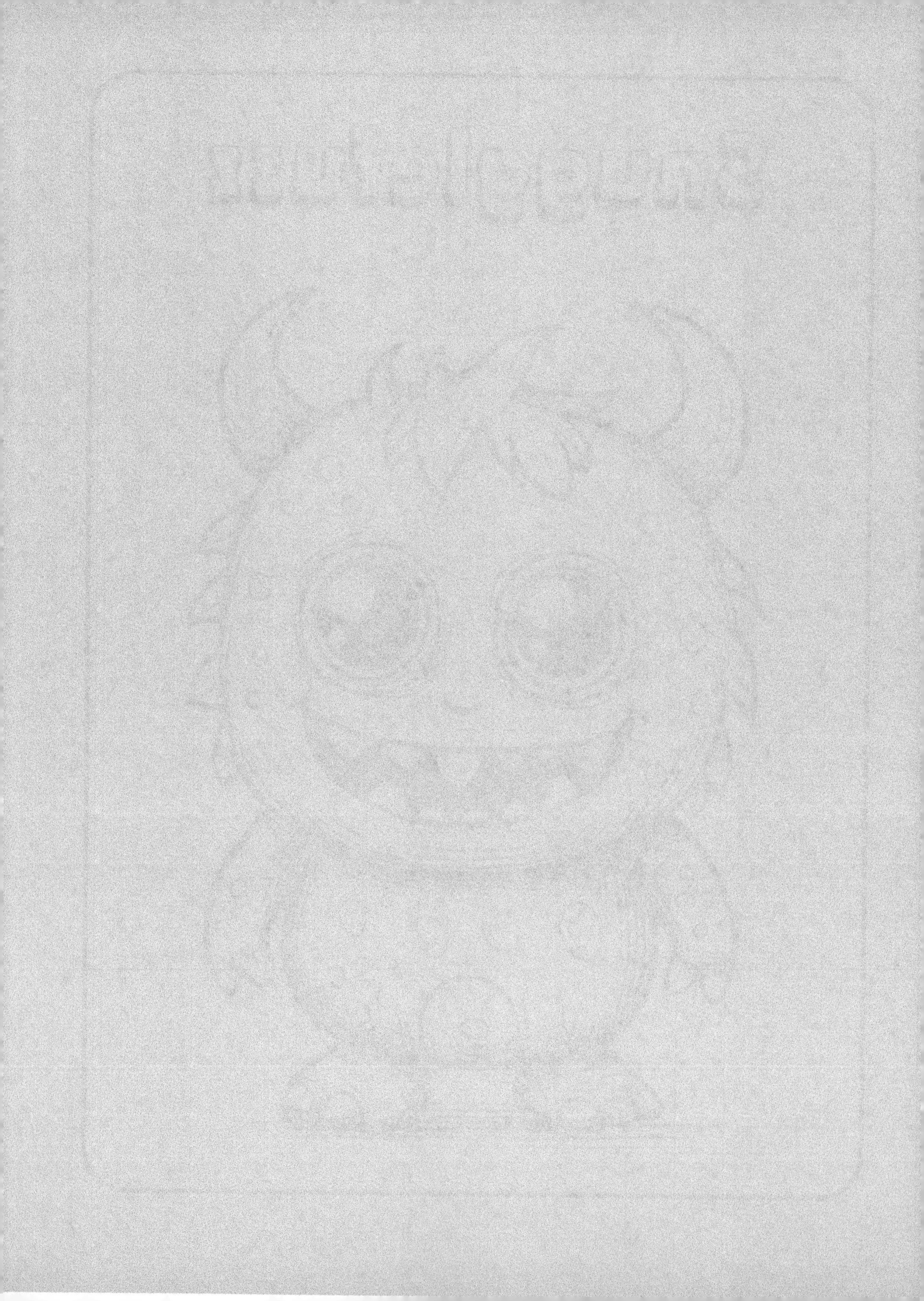

Squeakybounce

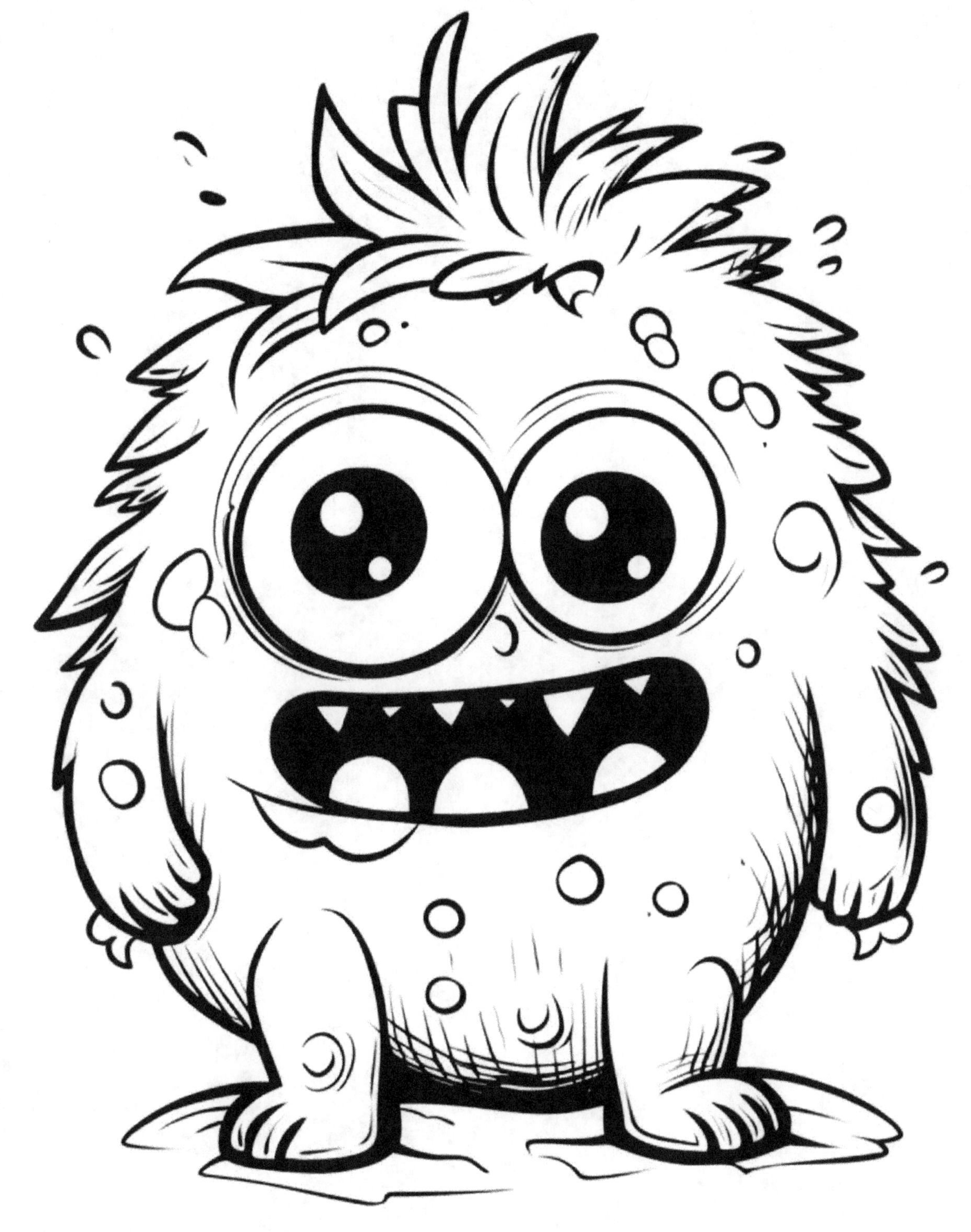

Jinglewhisk

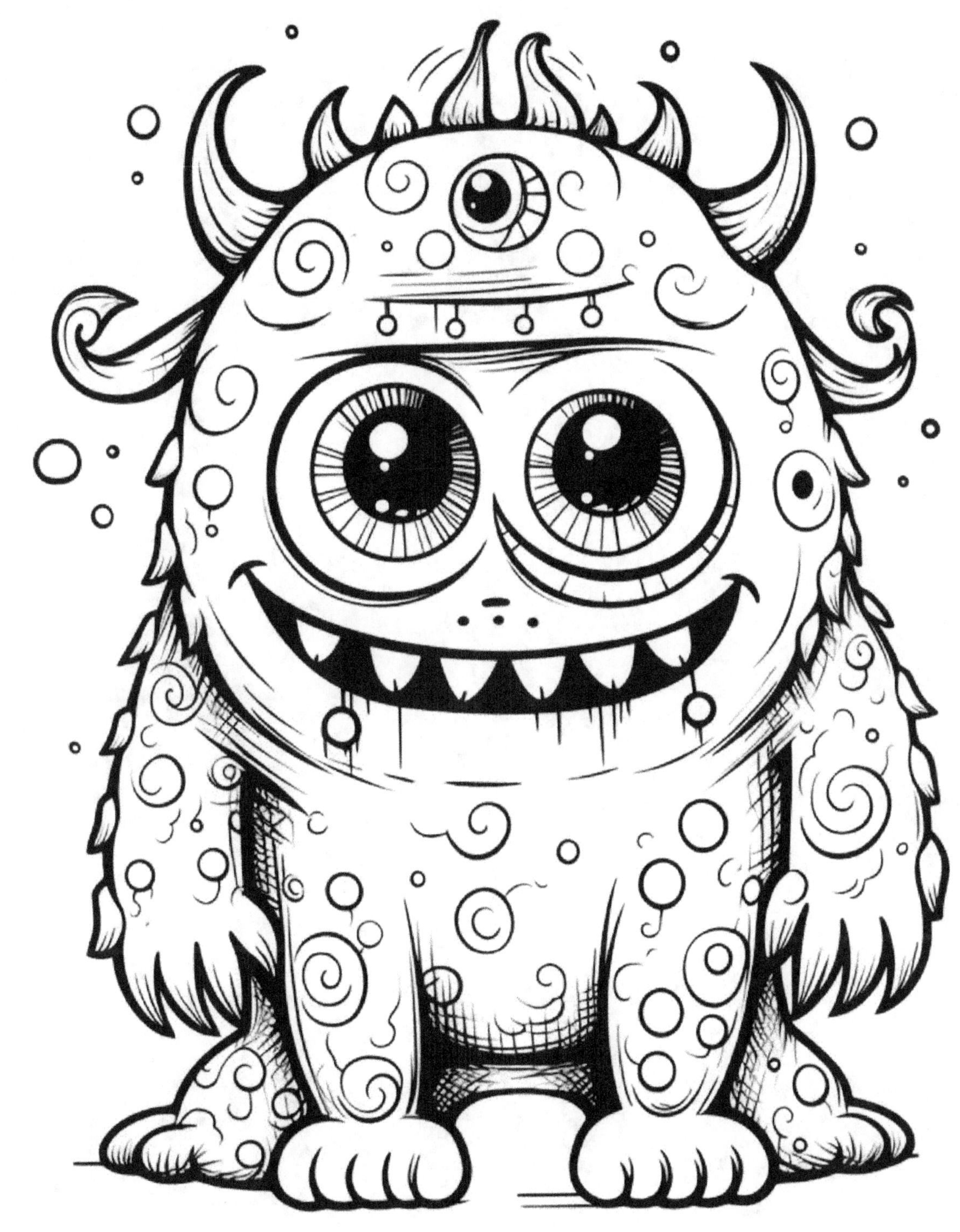

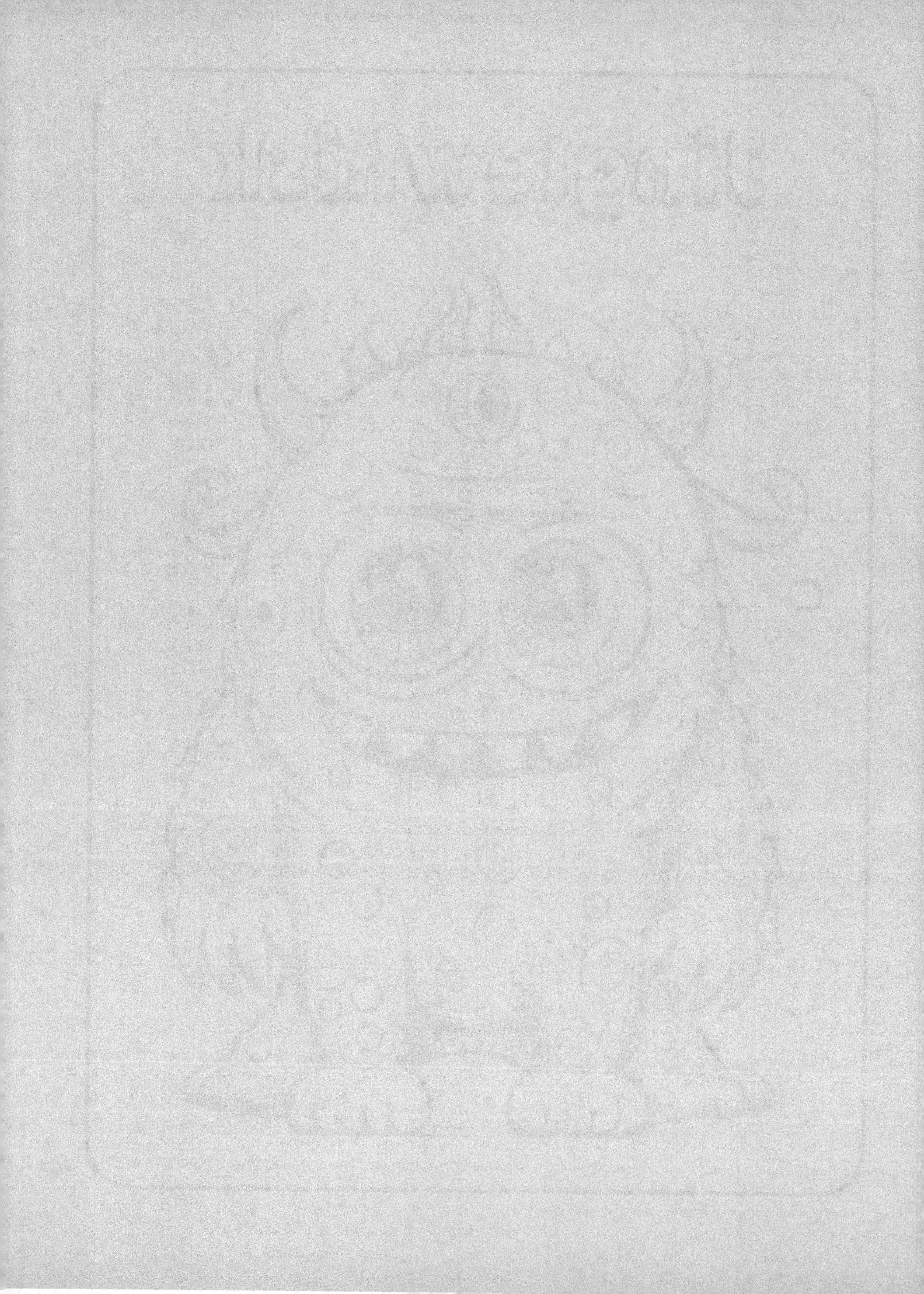

Puddlesnack

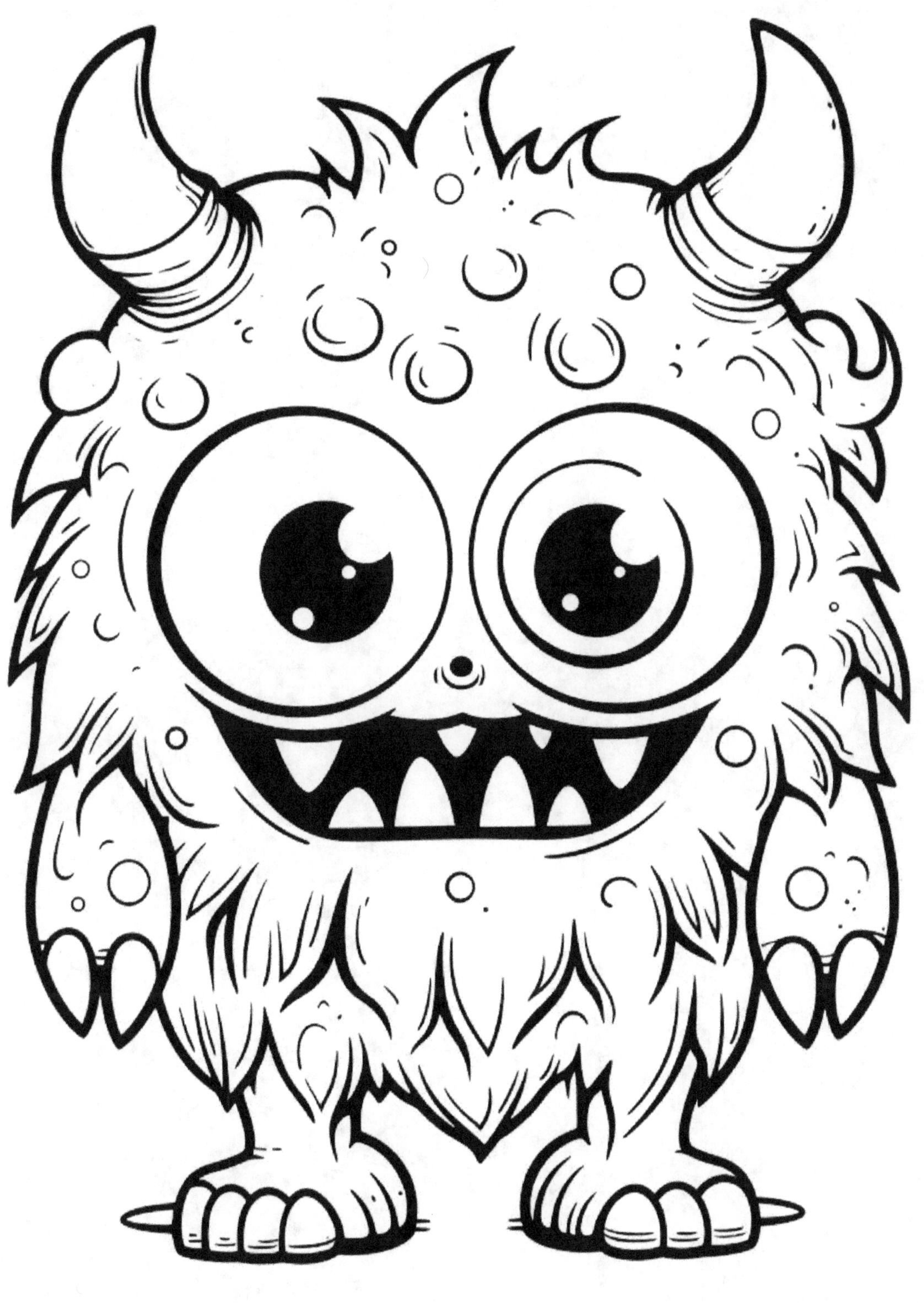

Dimplesnuggle

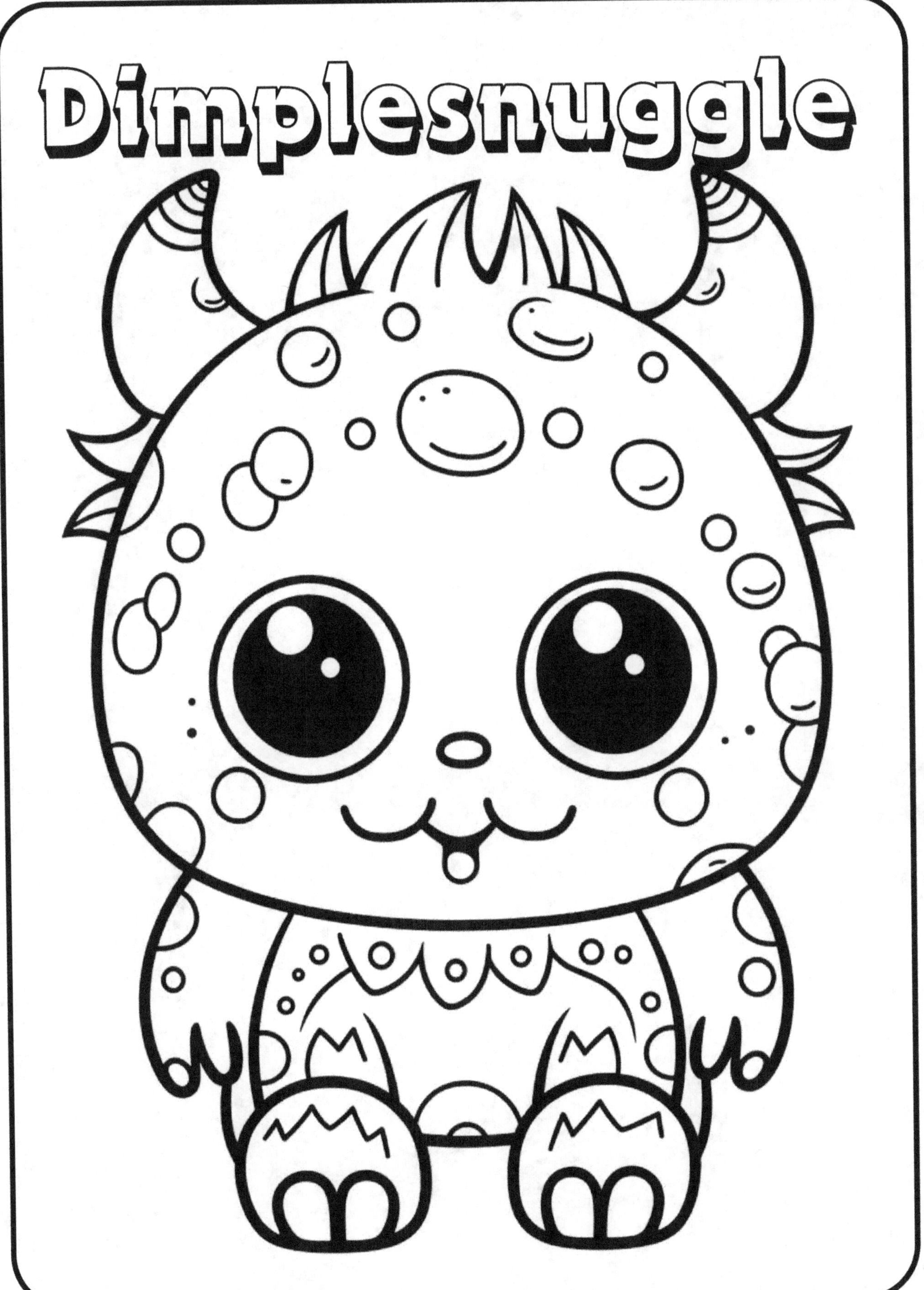

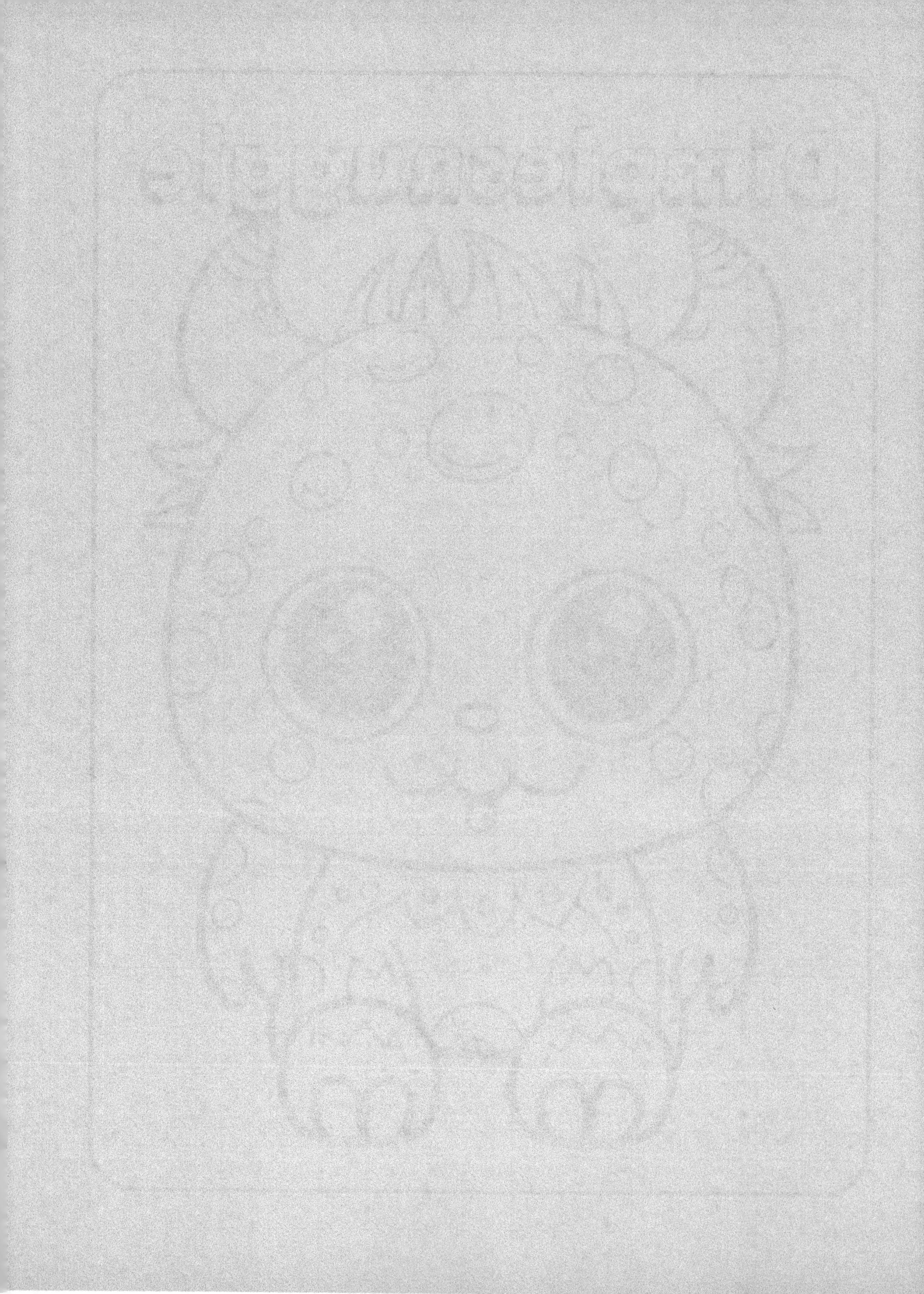

Wobblewhisk

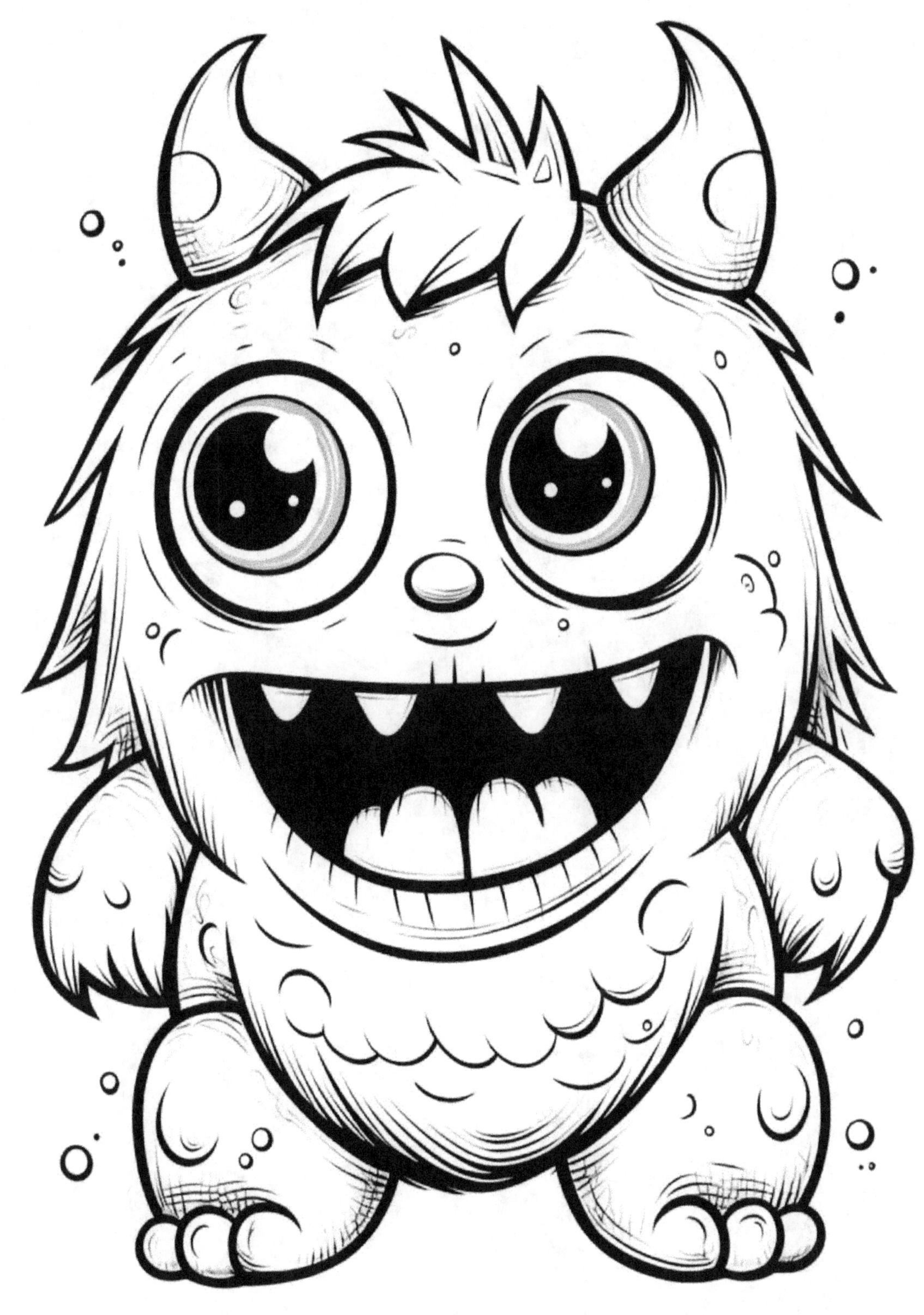

Zigglytwist

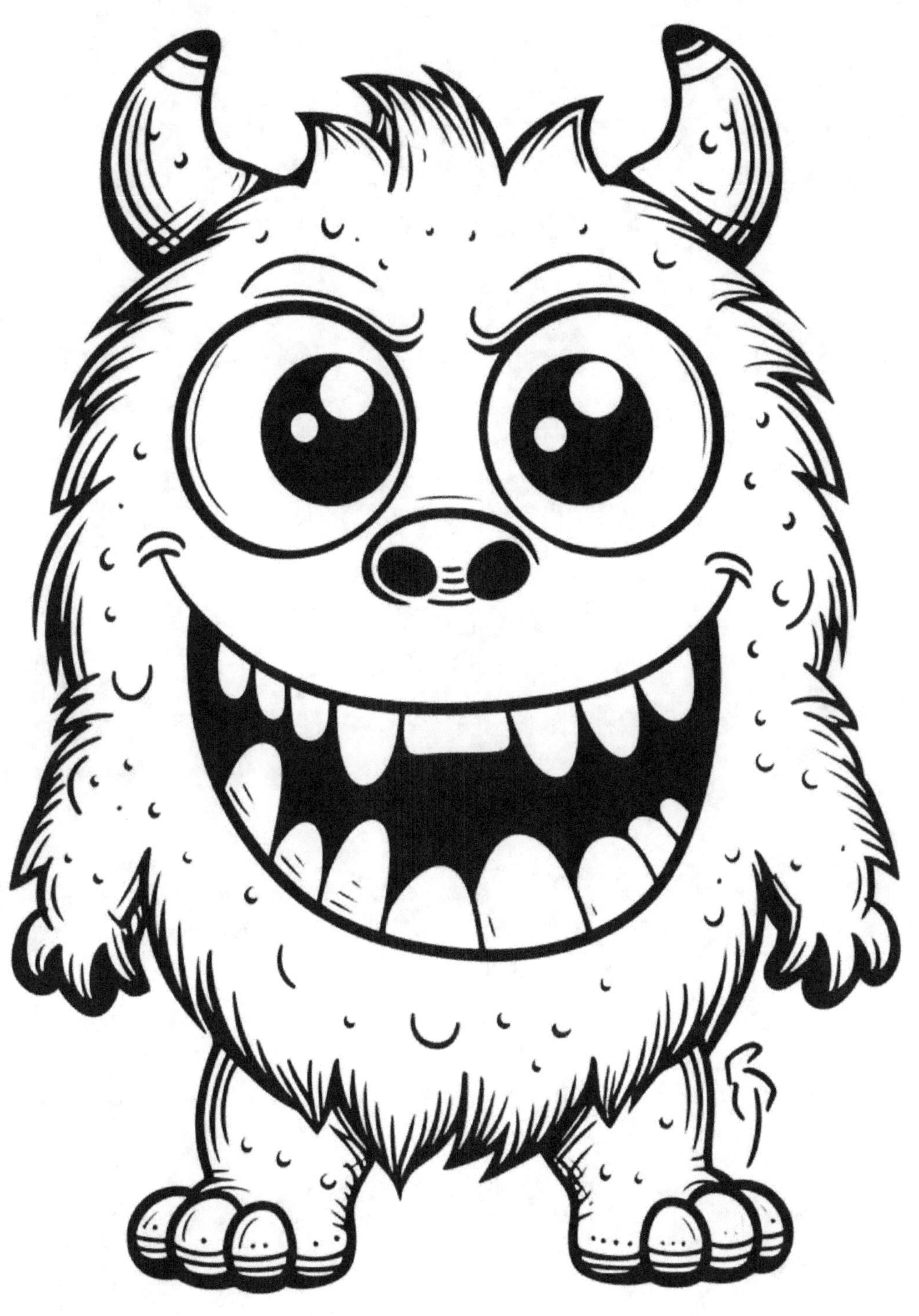

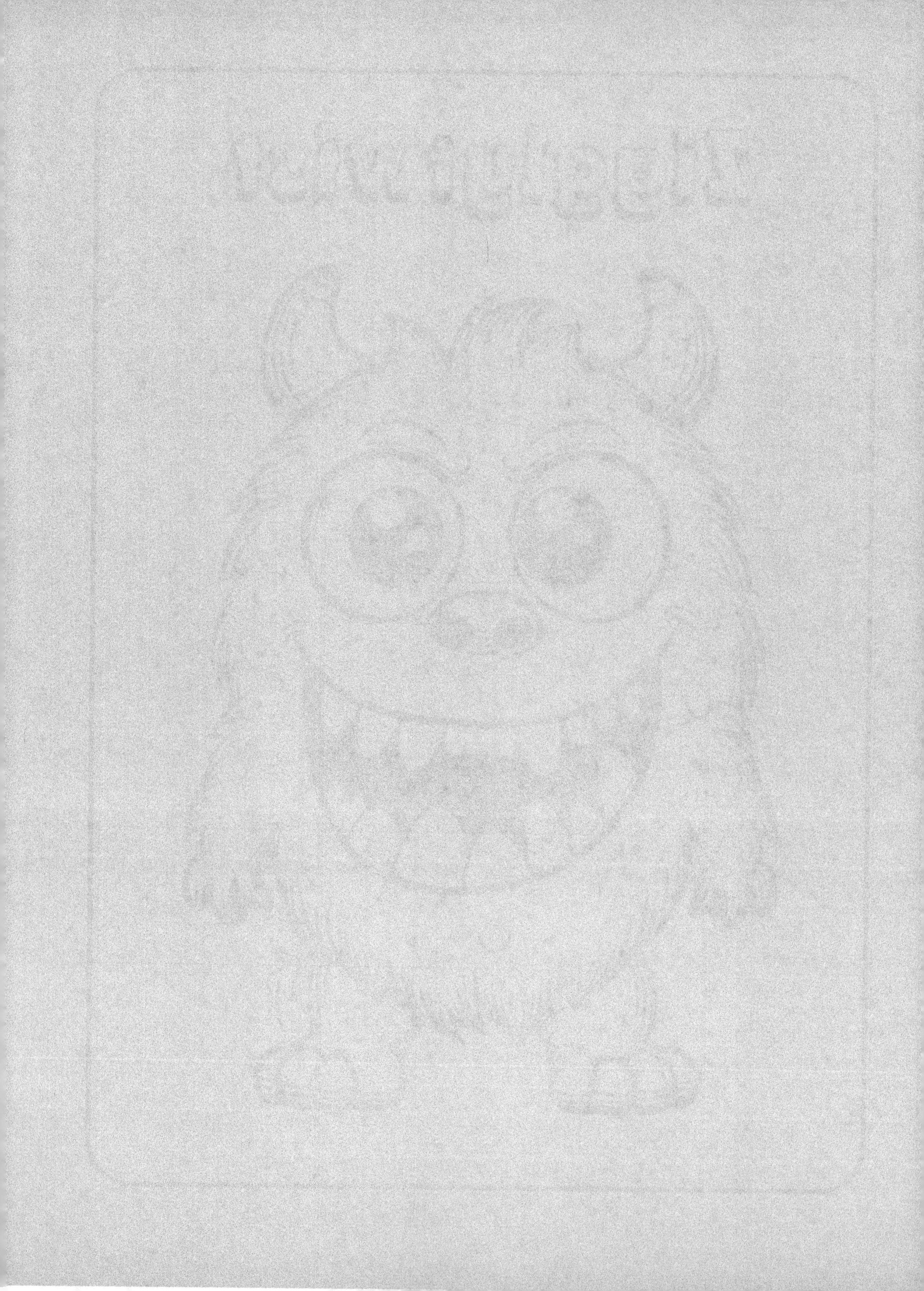

Sprinklesnack

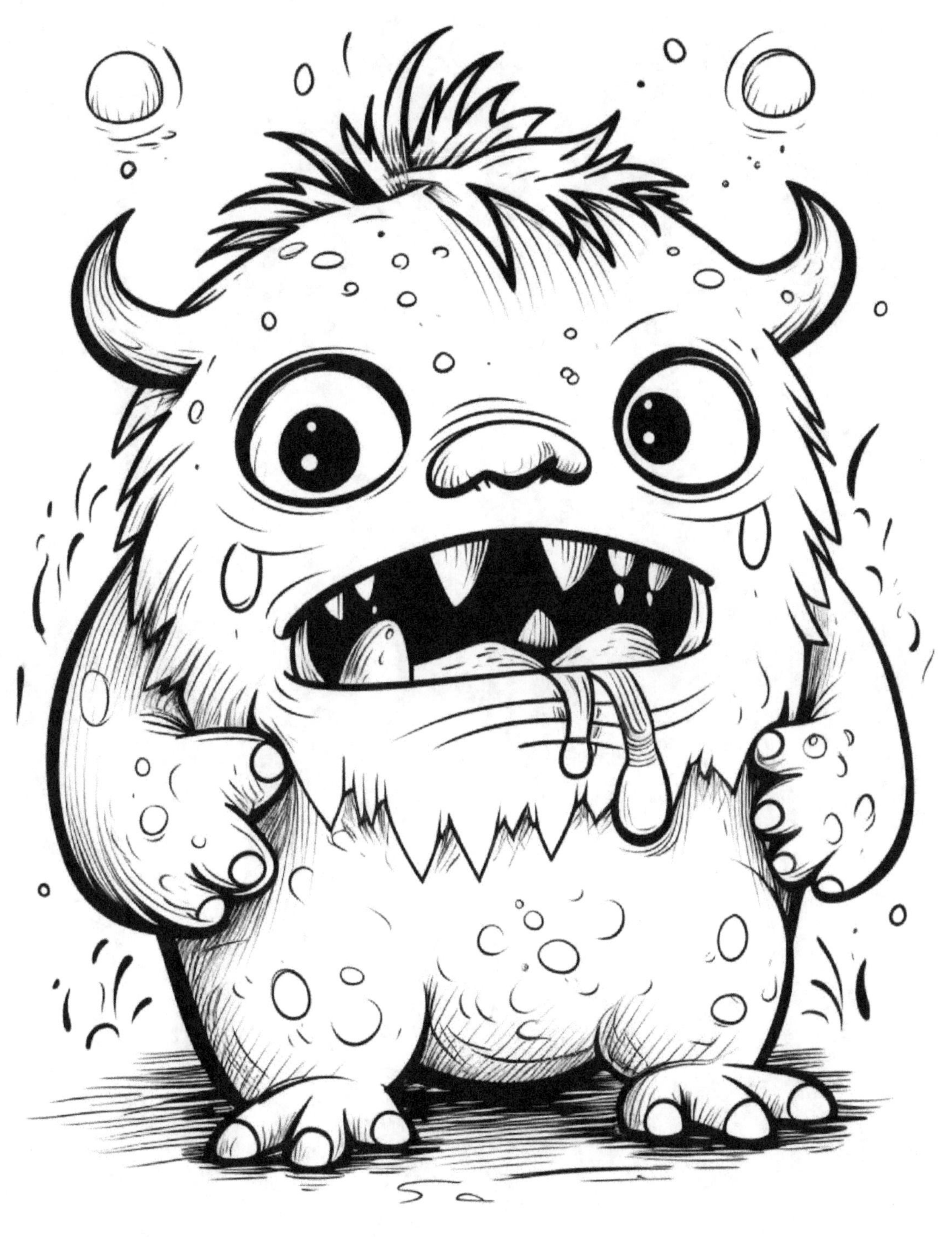

Snickerbounce

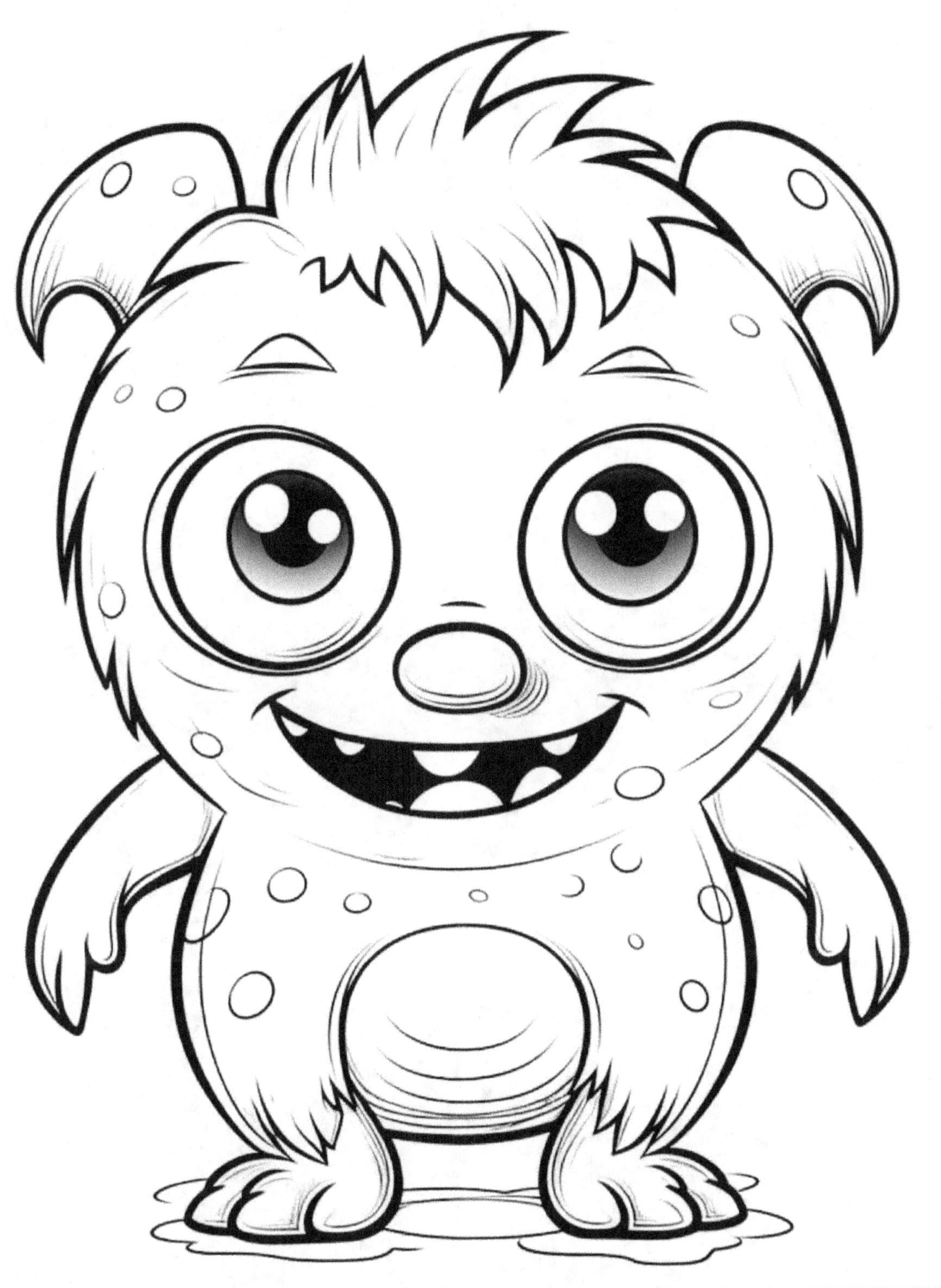

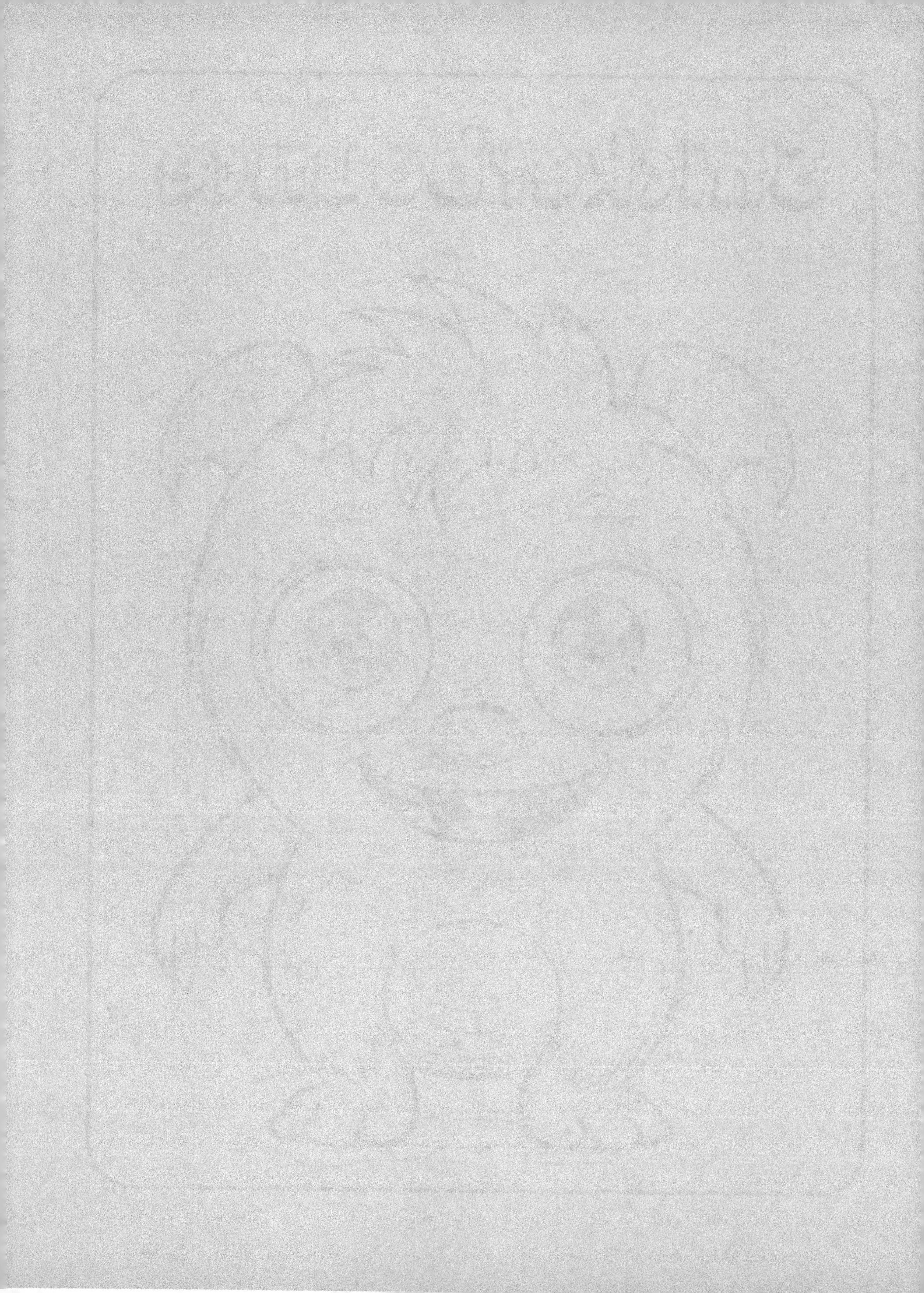

Bumbletwirl

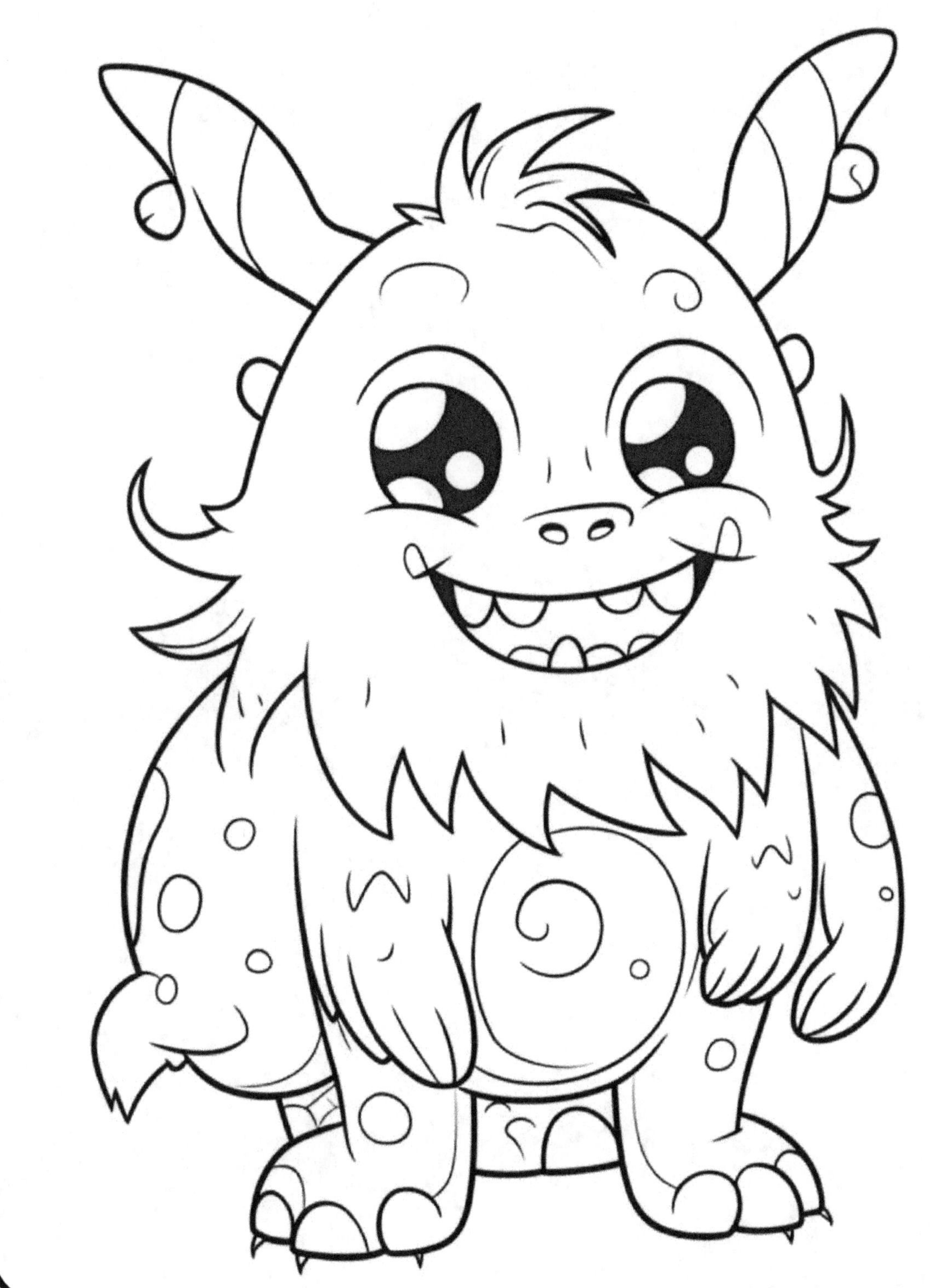

Cuddlewhisk

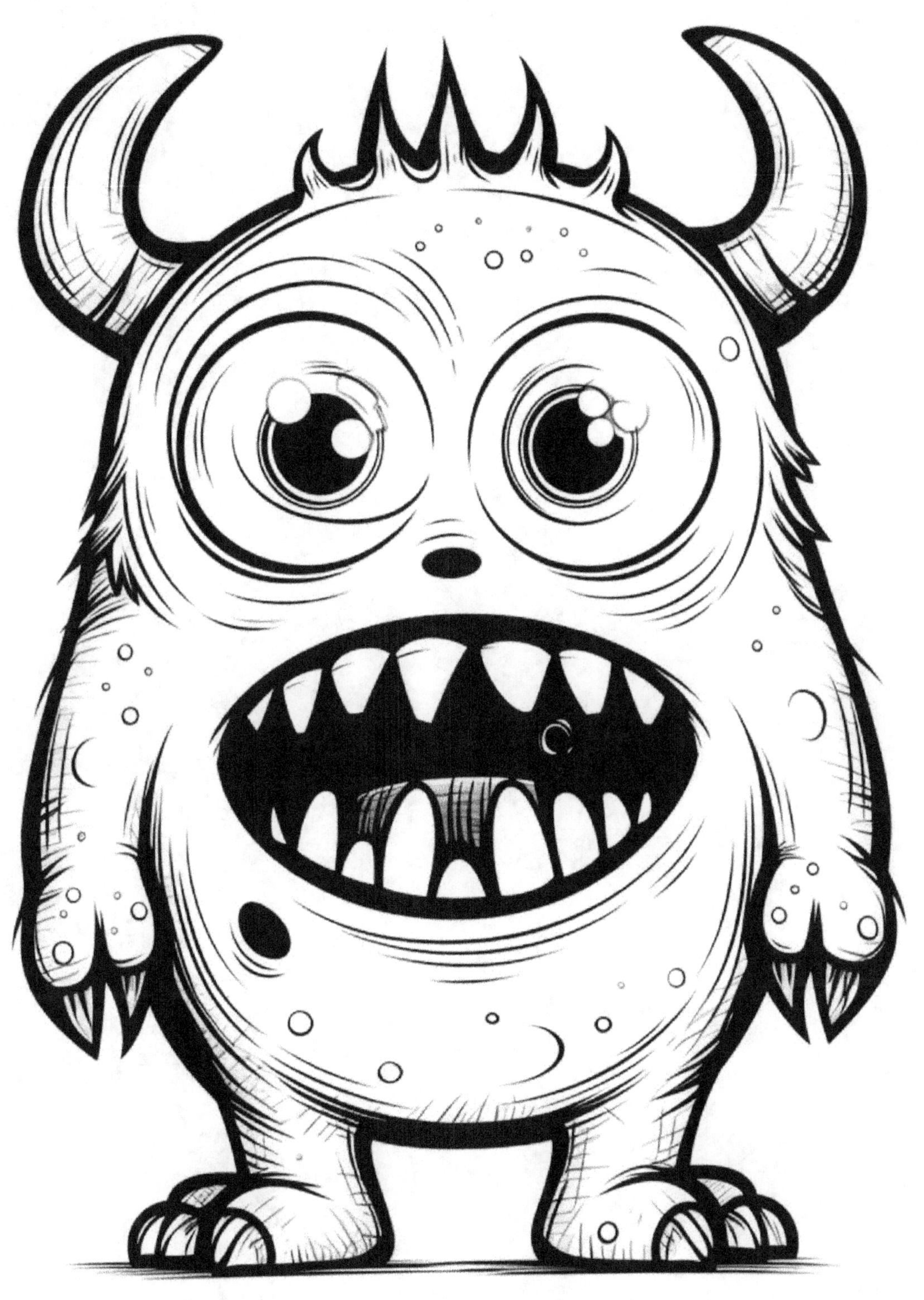

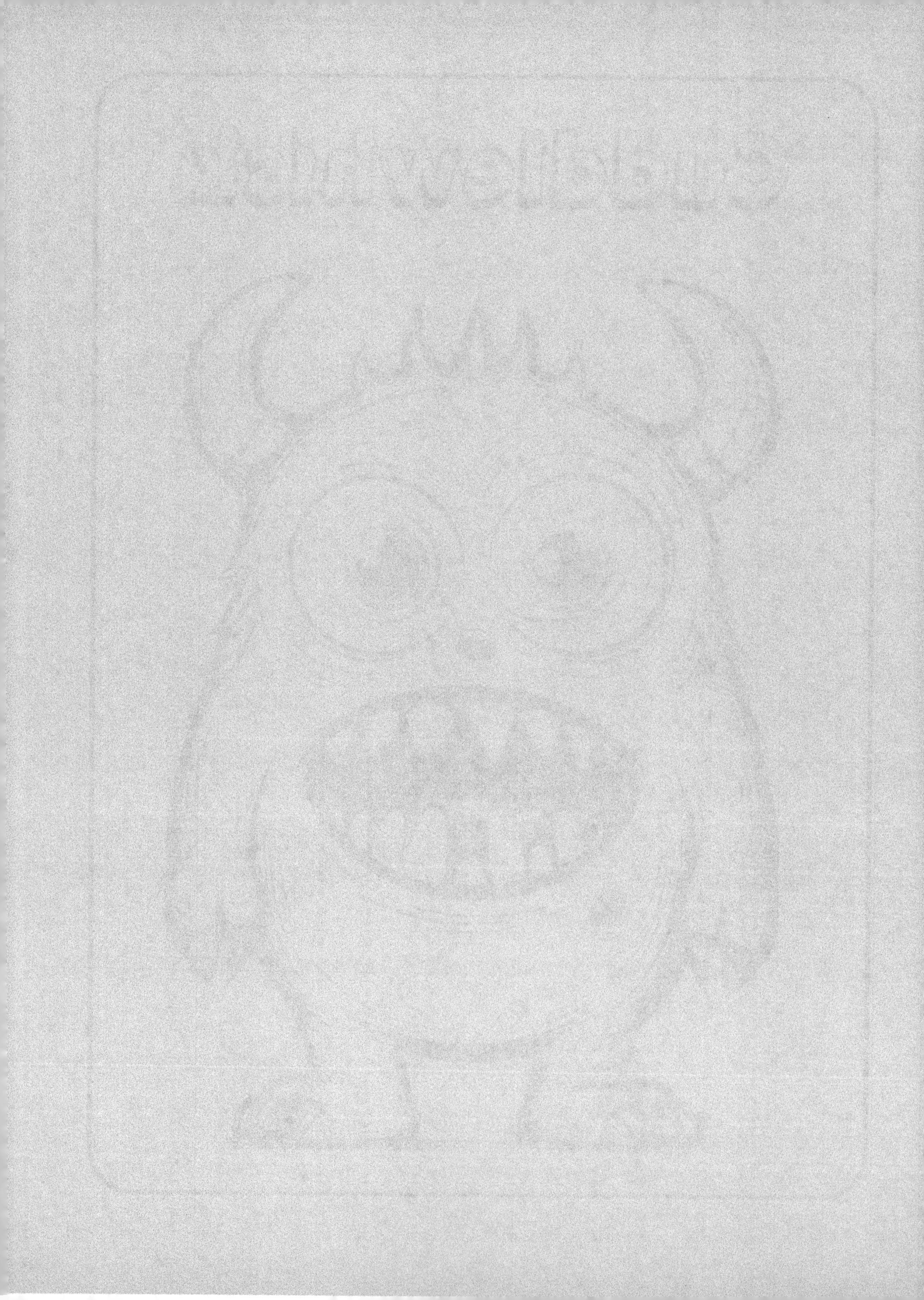

Wigglywobble

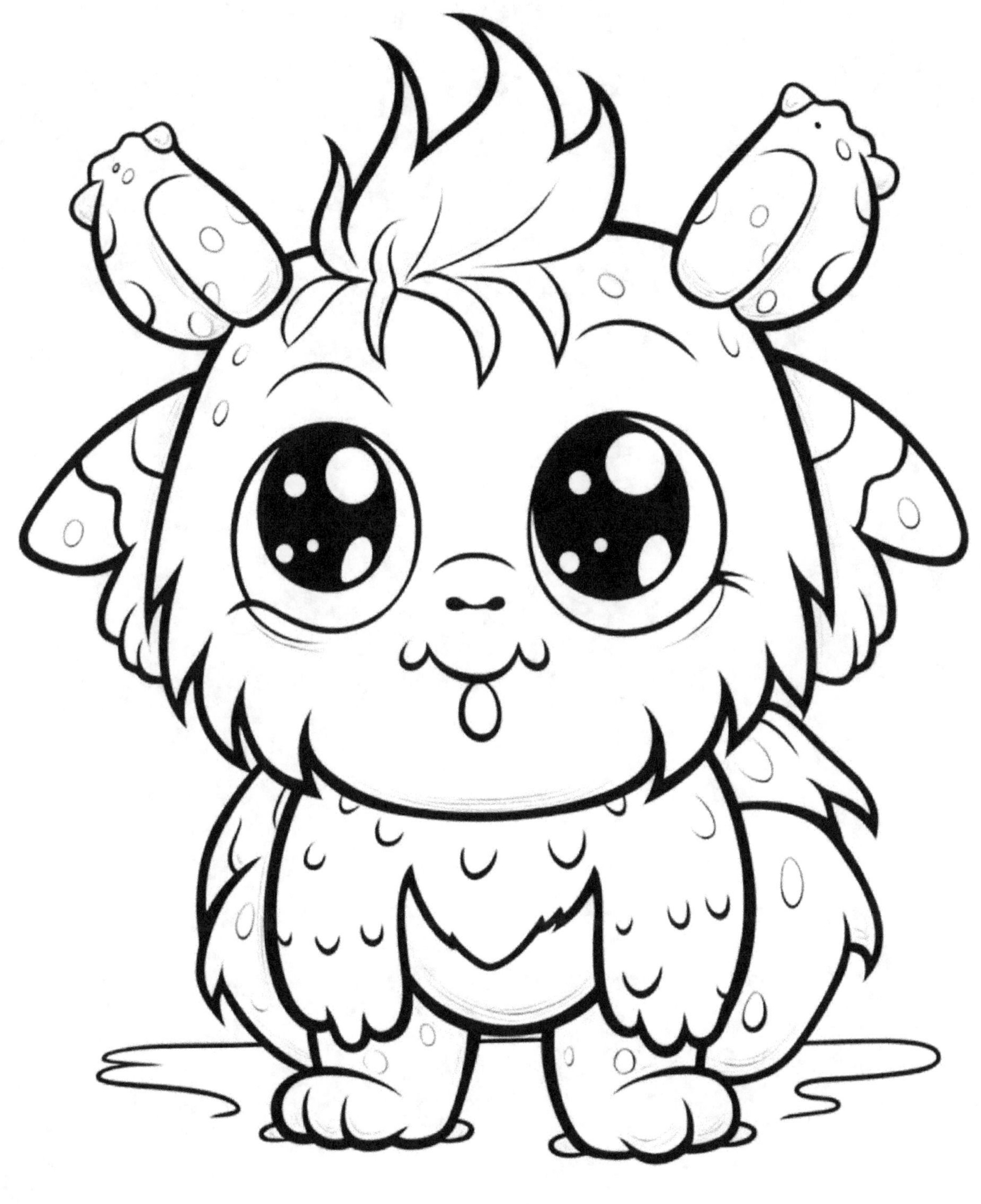

Twinklebounce

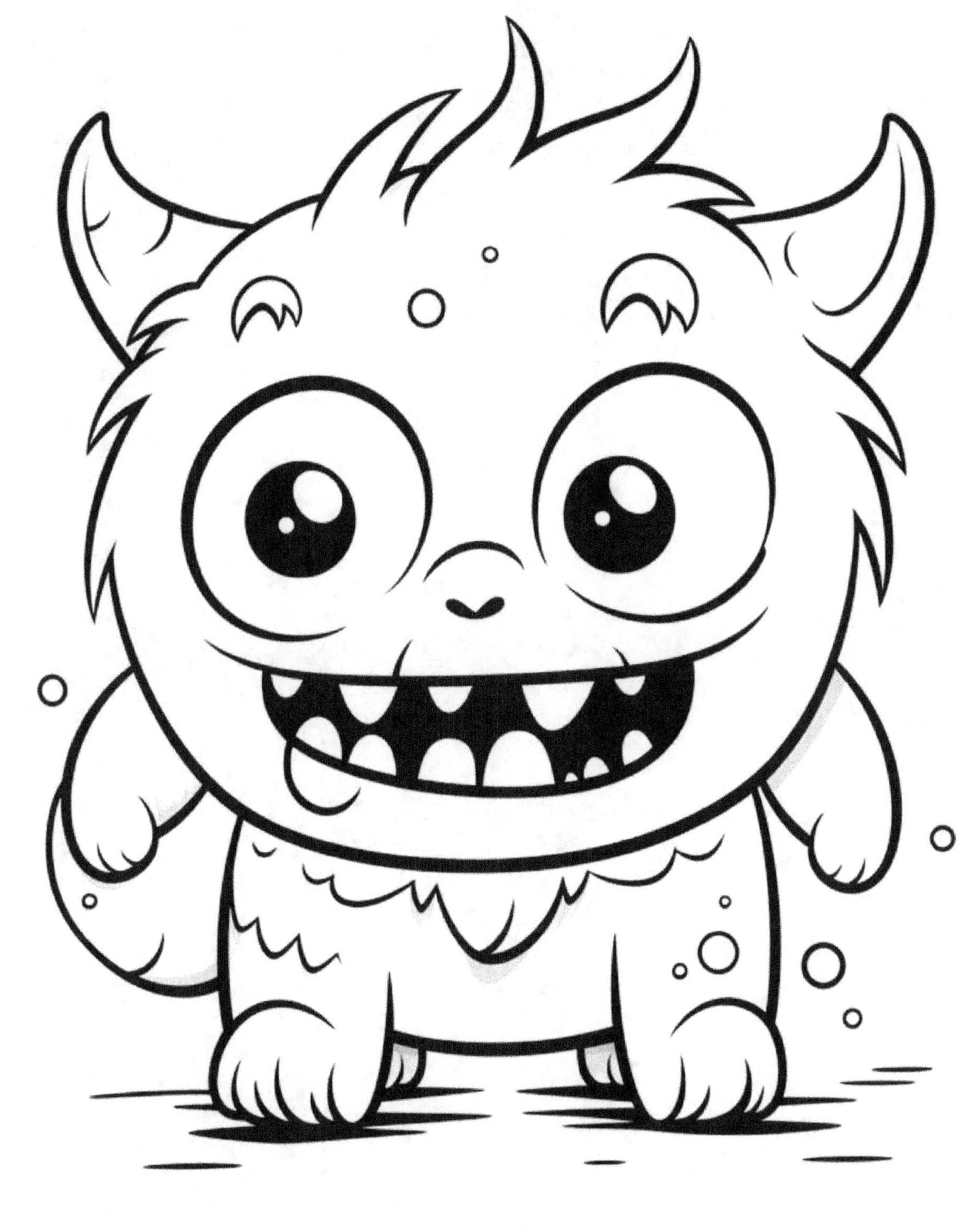

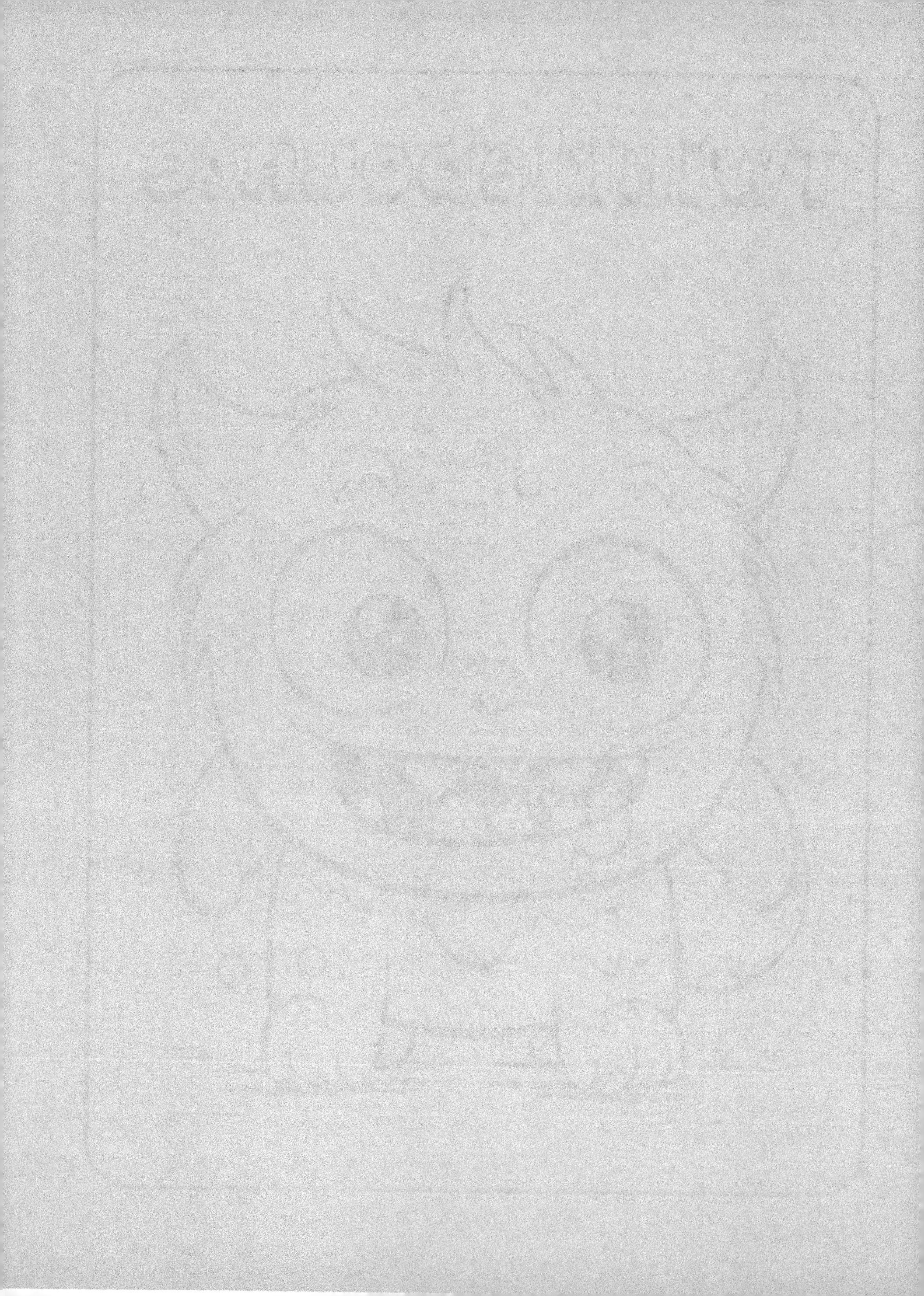

Glimmersnuggle

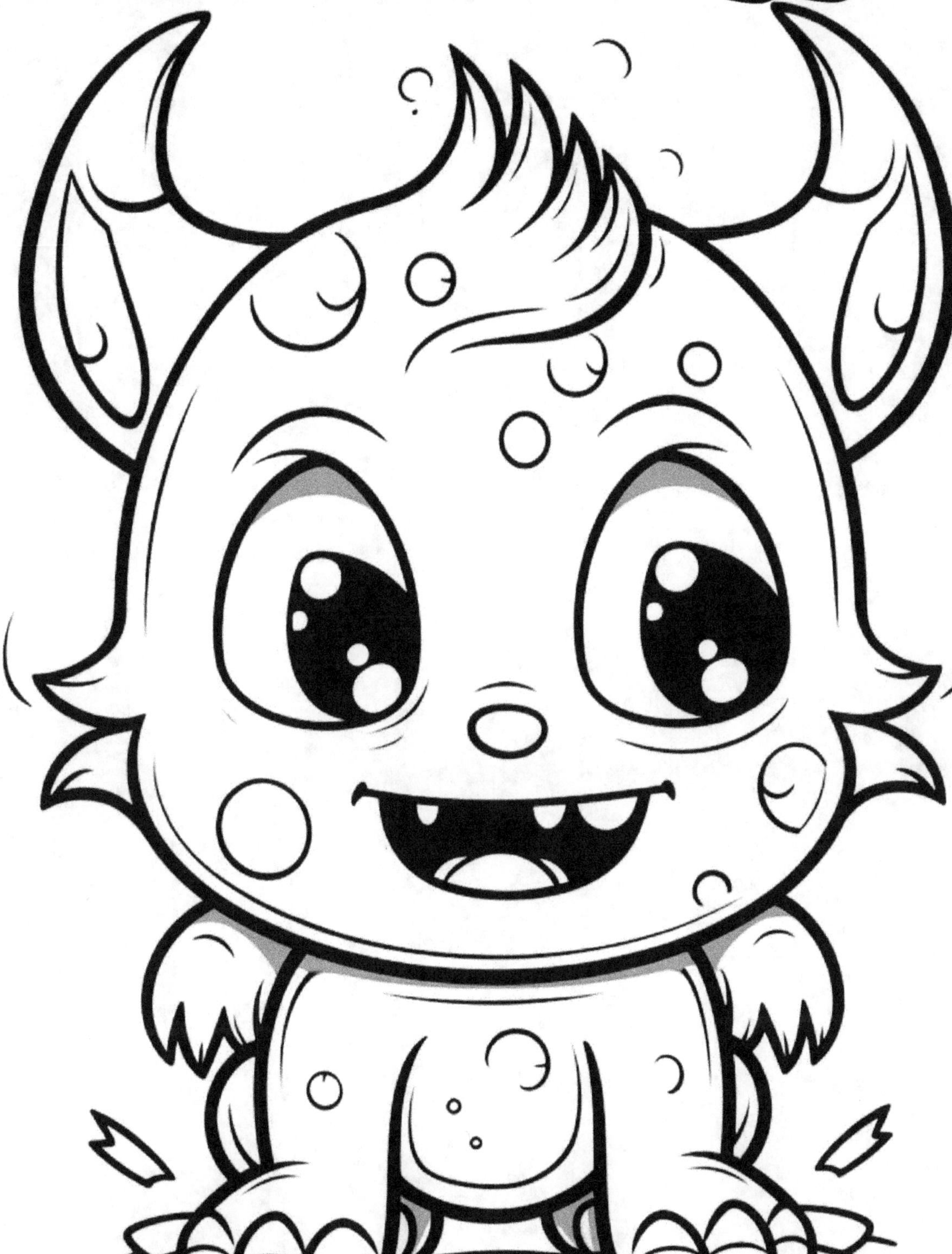

Doodlebop

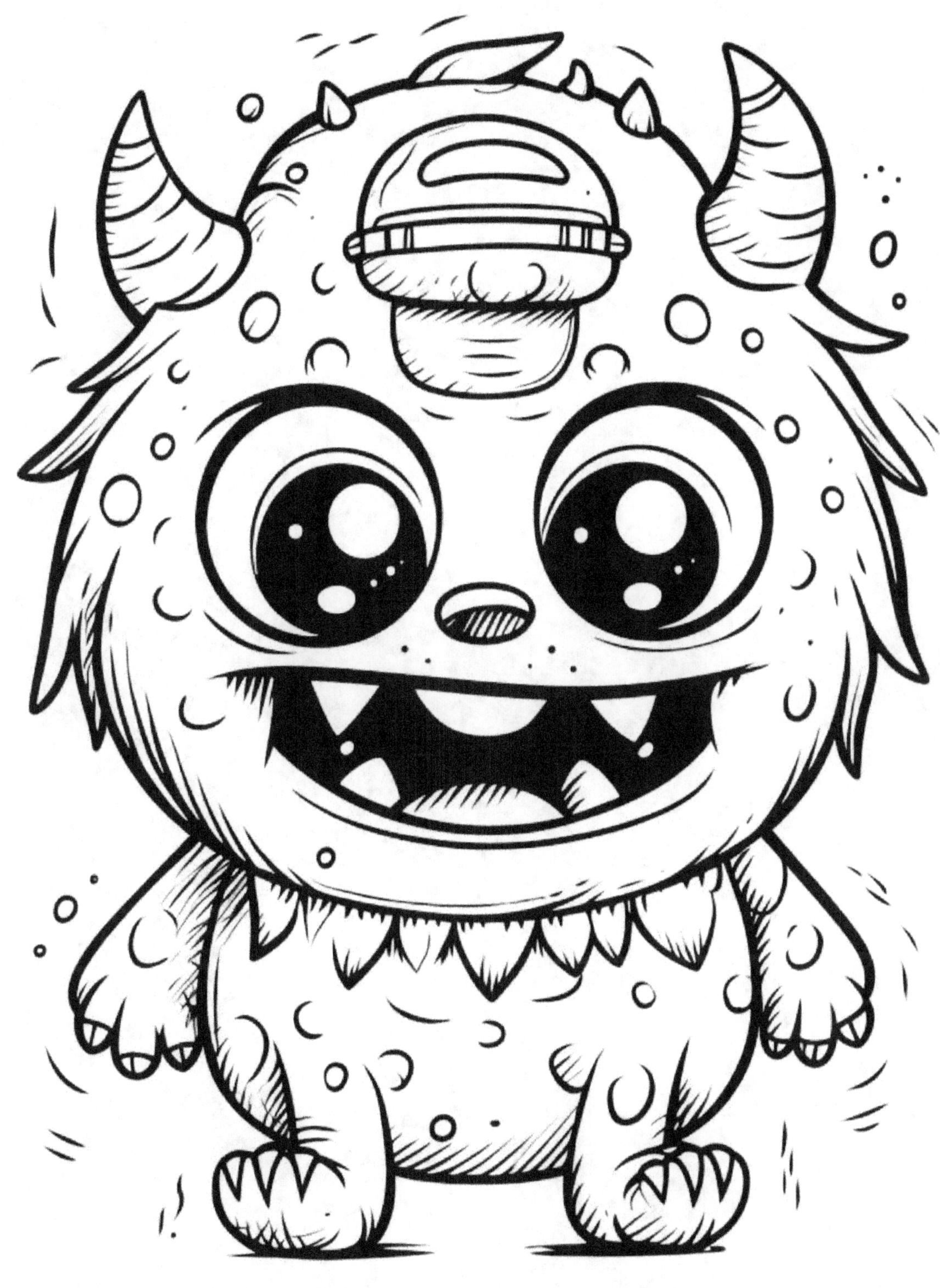

Squeakydoo

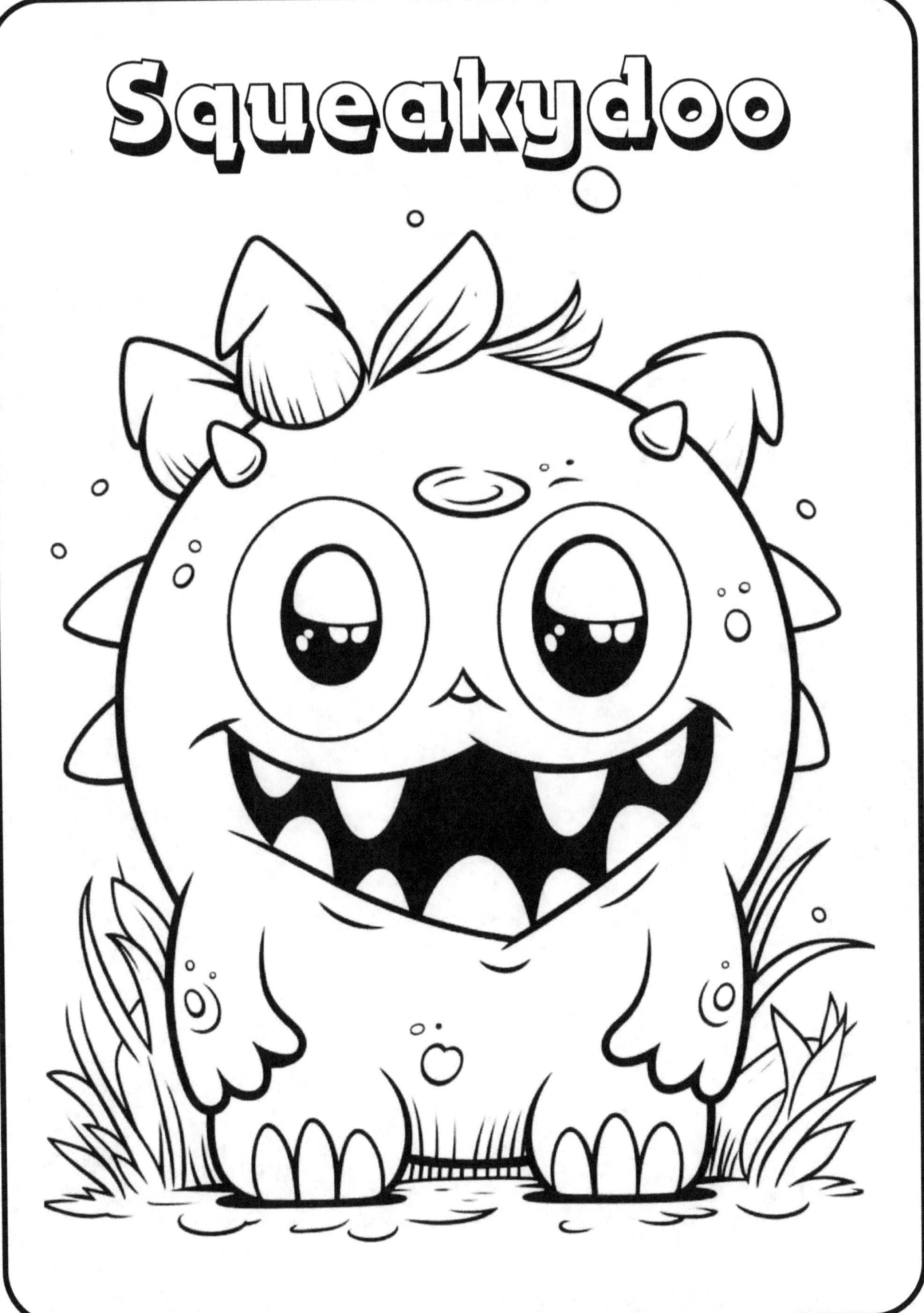

Furrywhirl

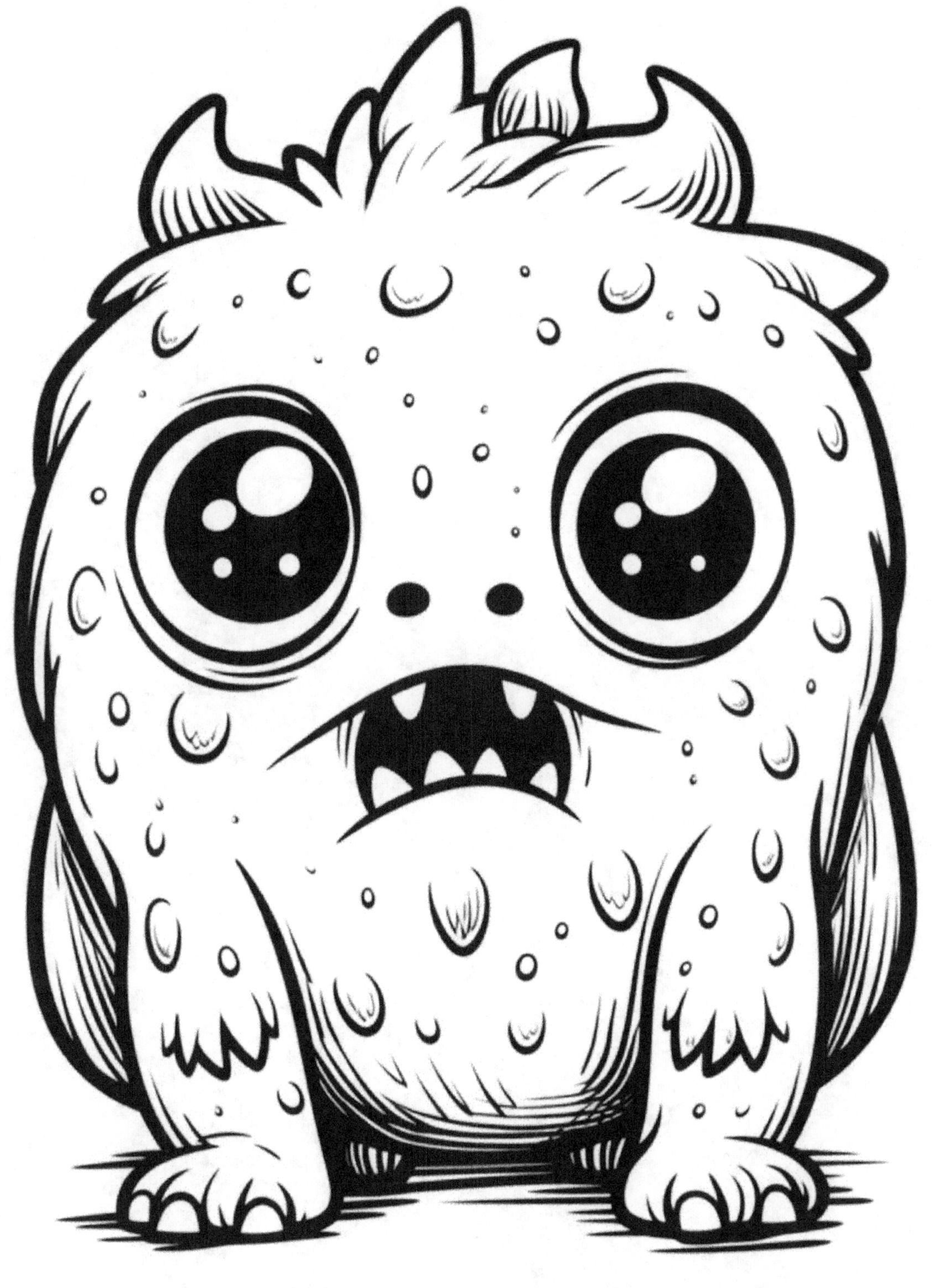

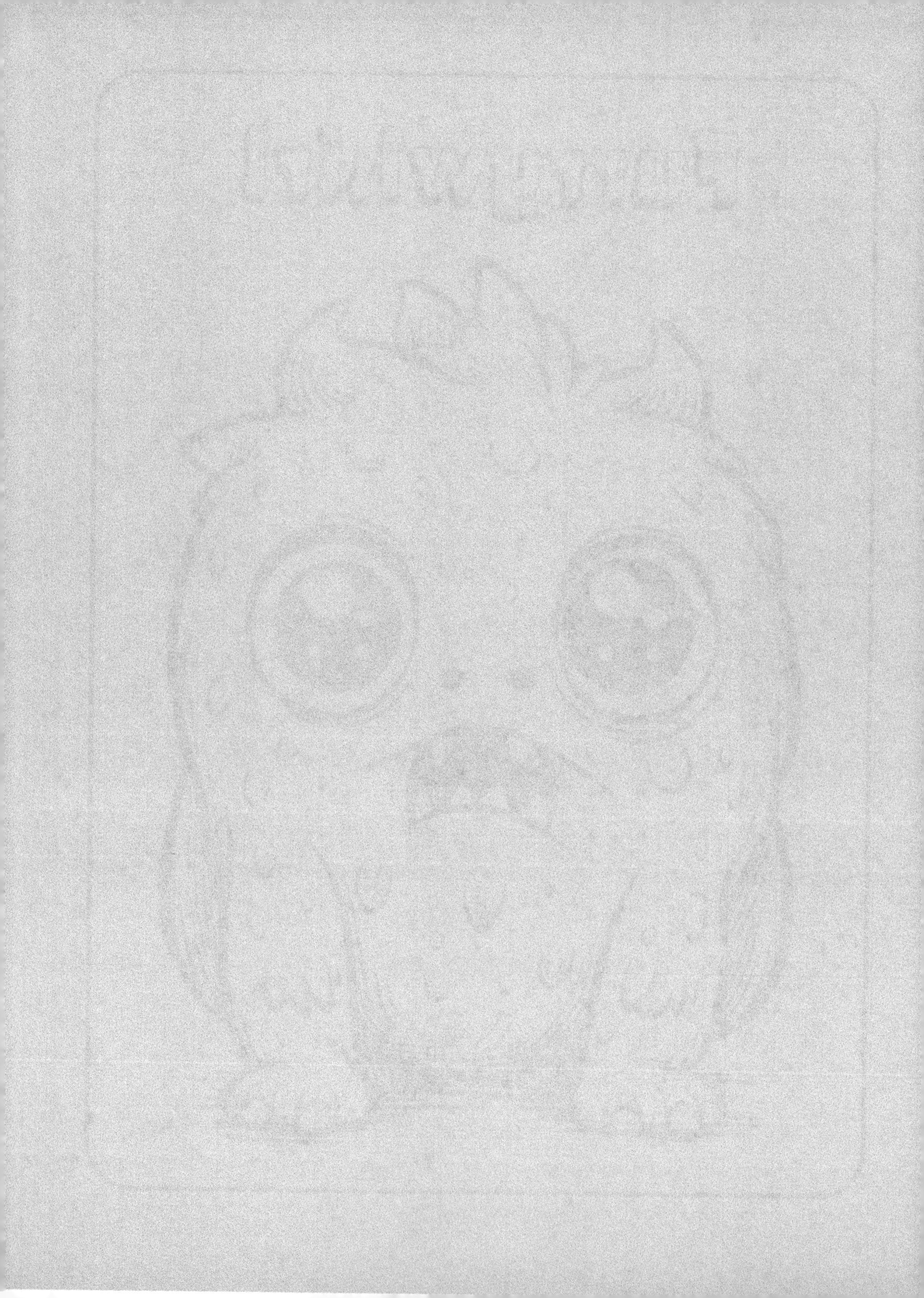

Snickerwhisk

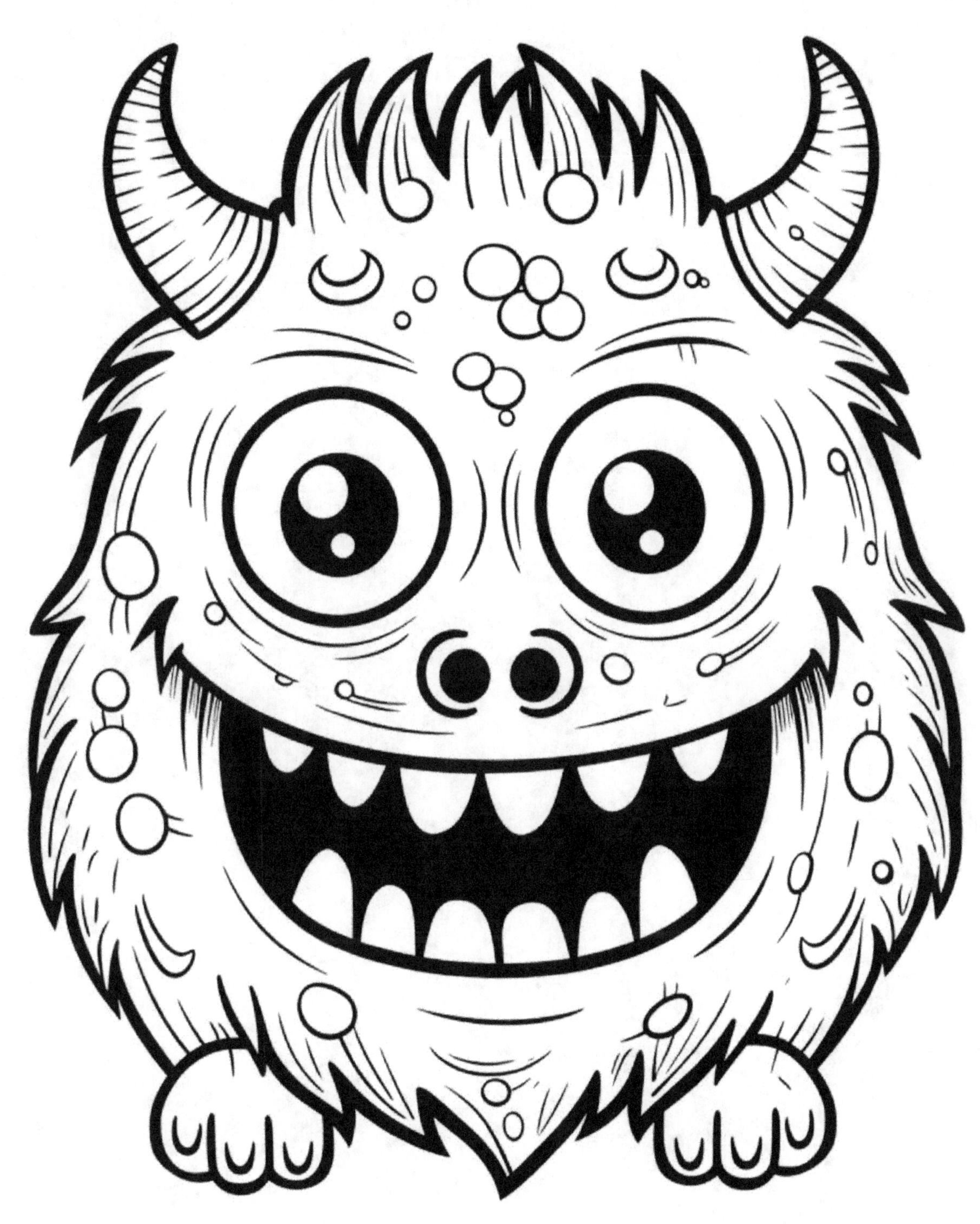

Gigglyfuzz

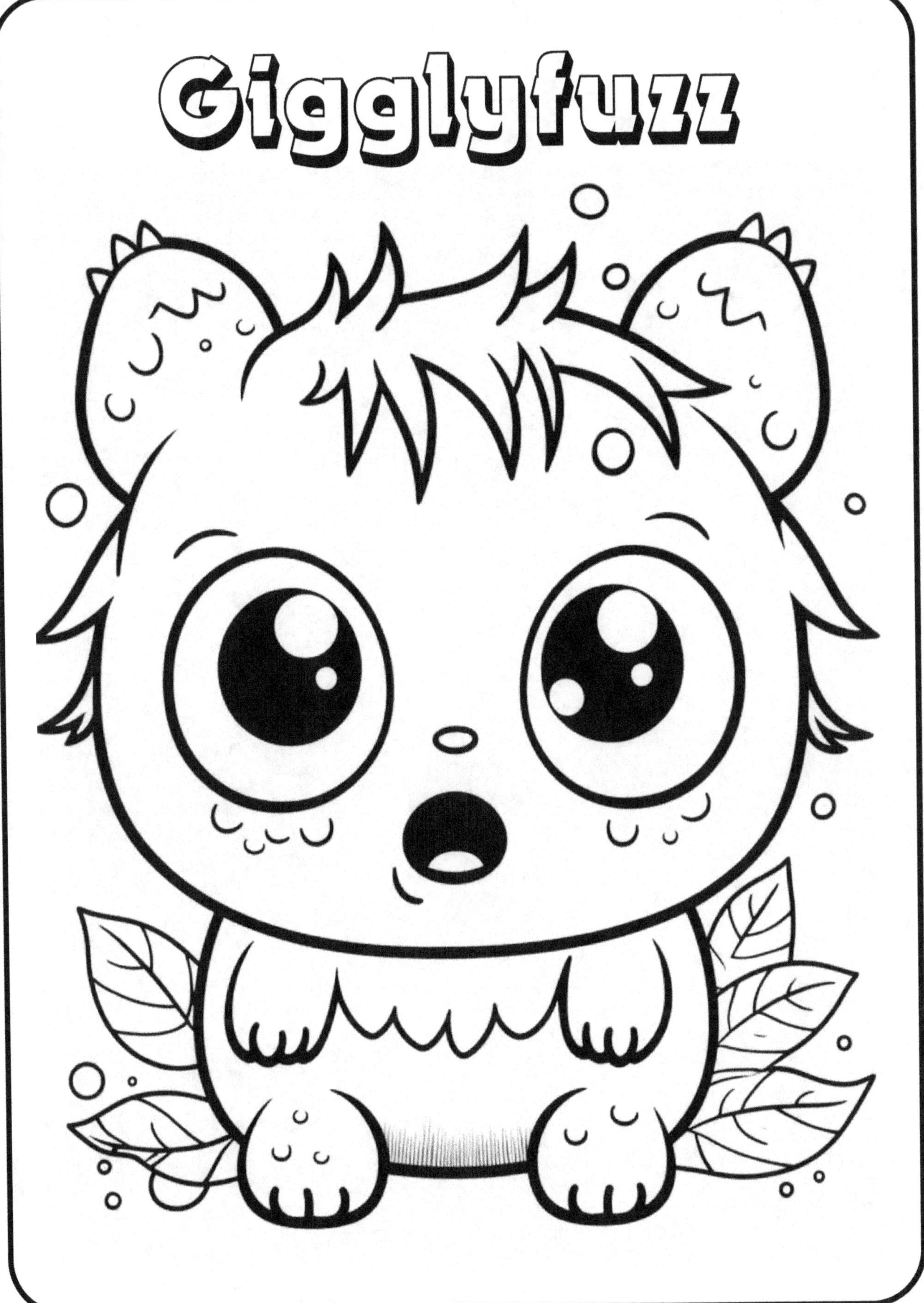

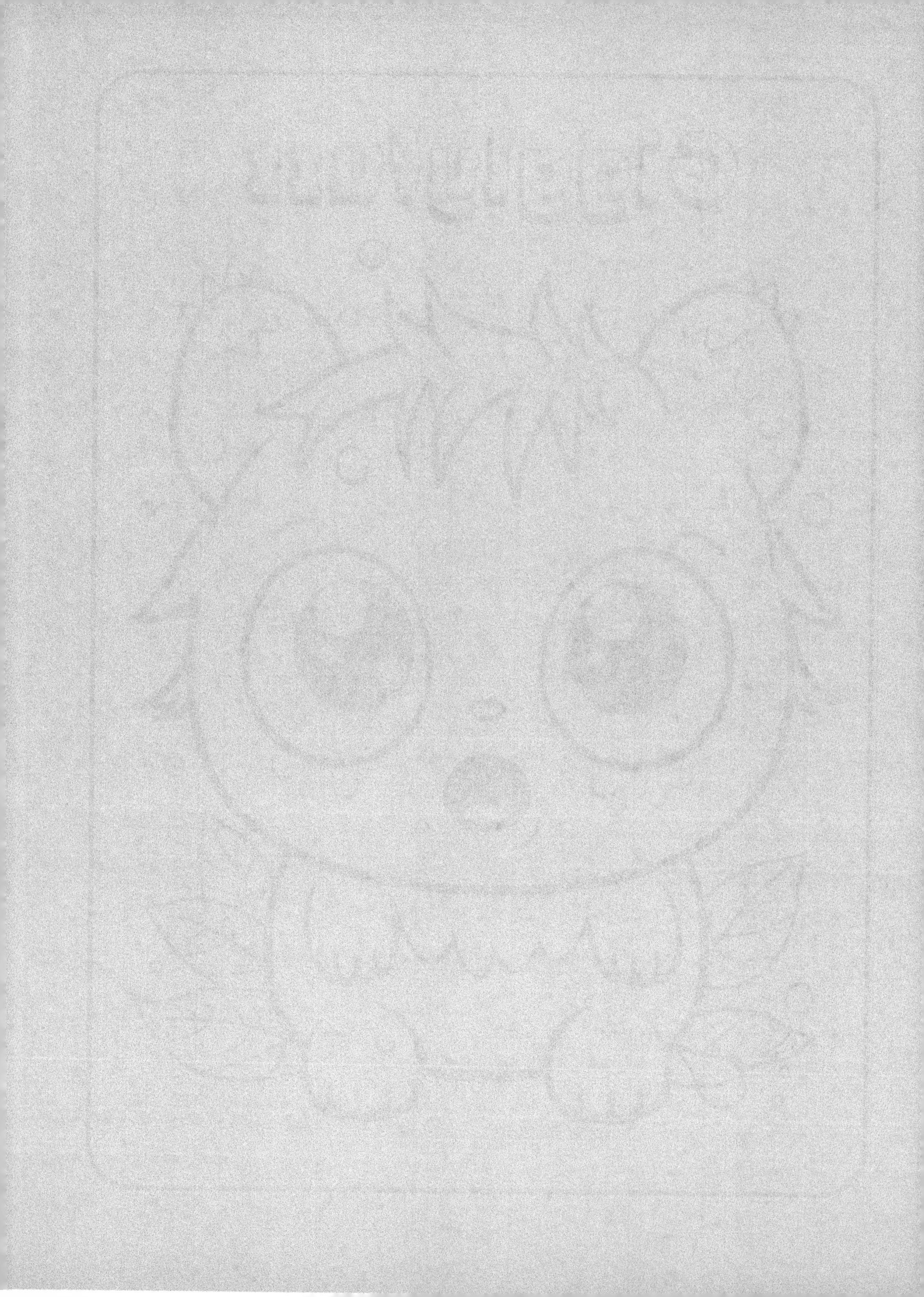

Snugglebounce

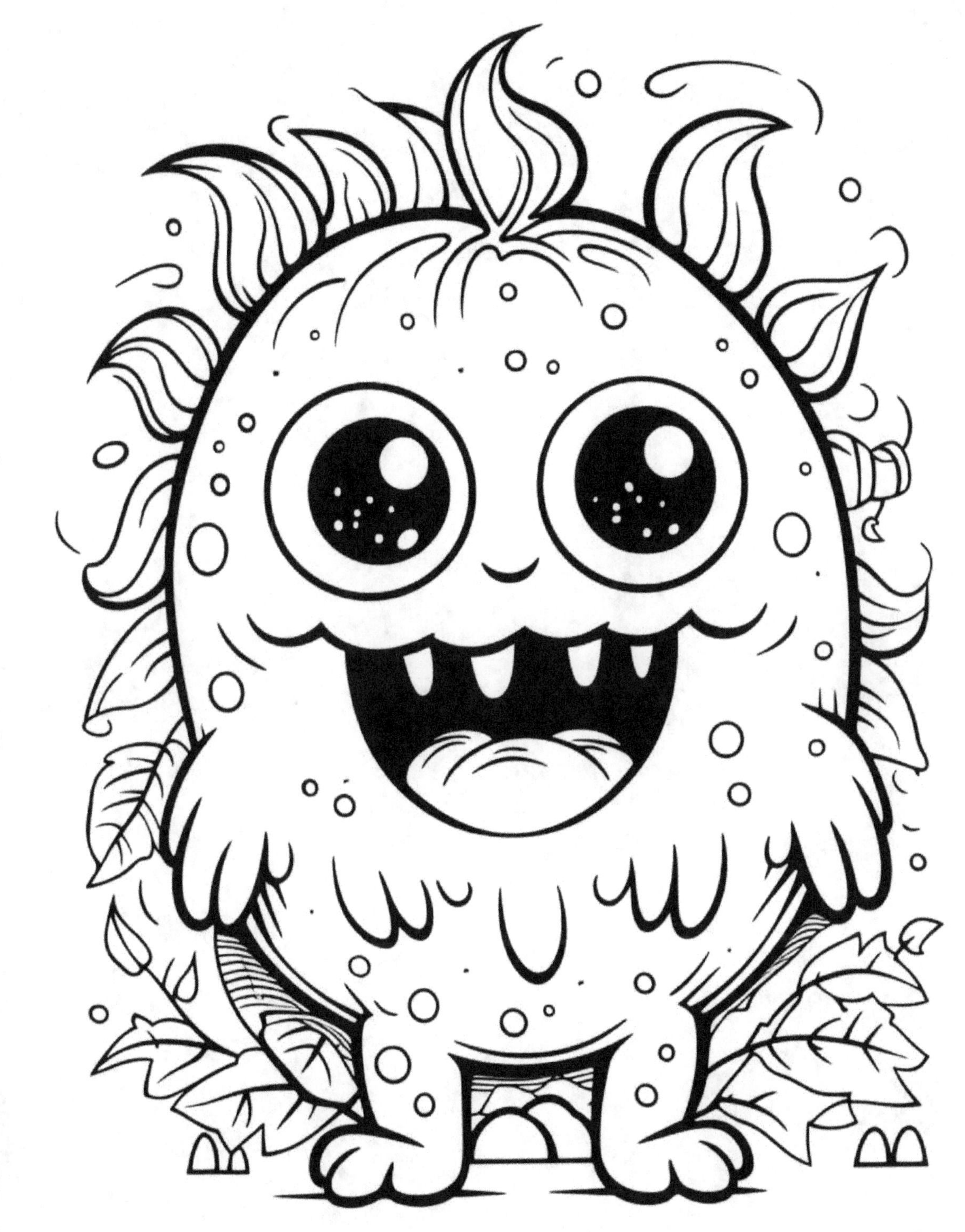

Wobblewhisk

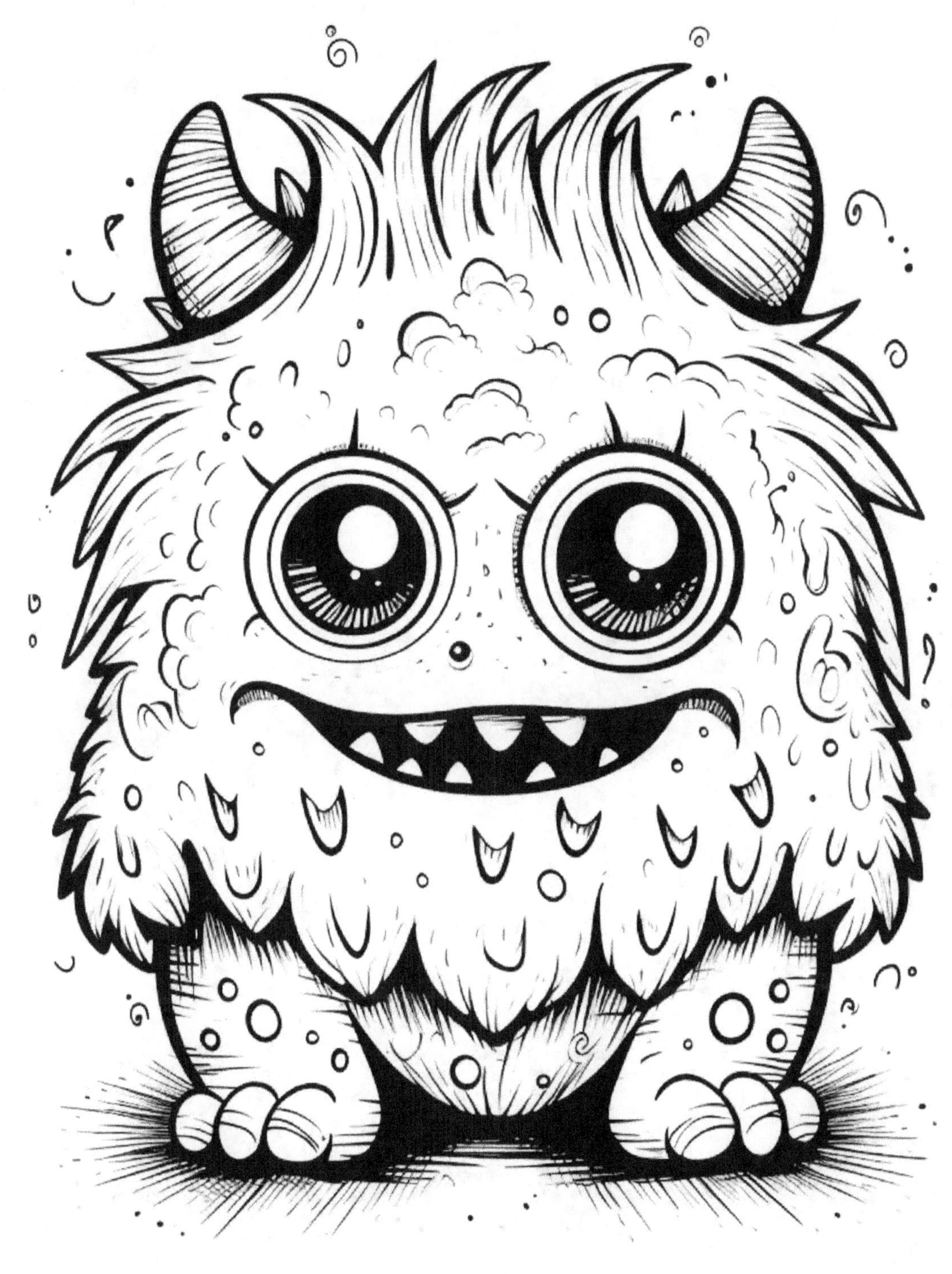

Dimplesnack

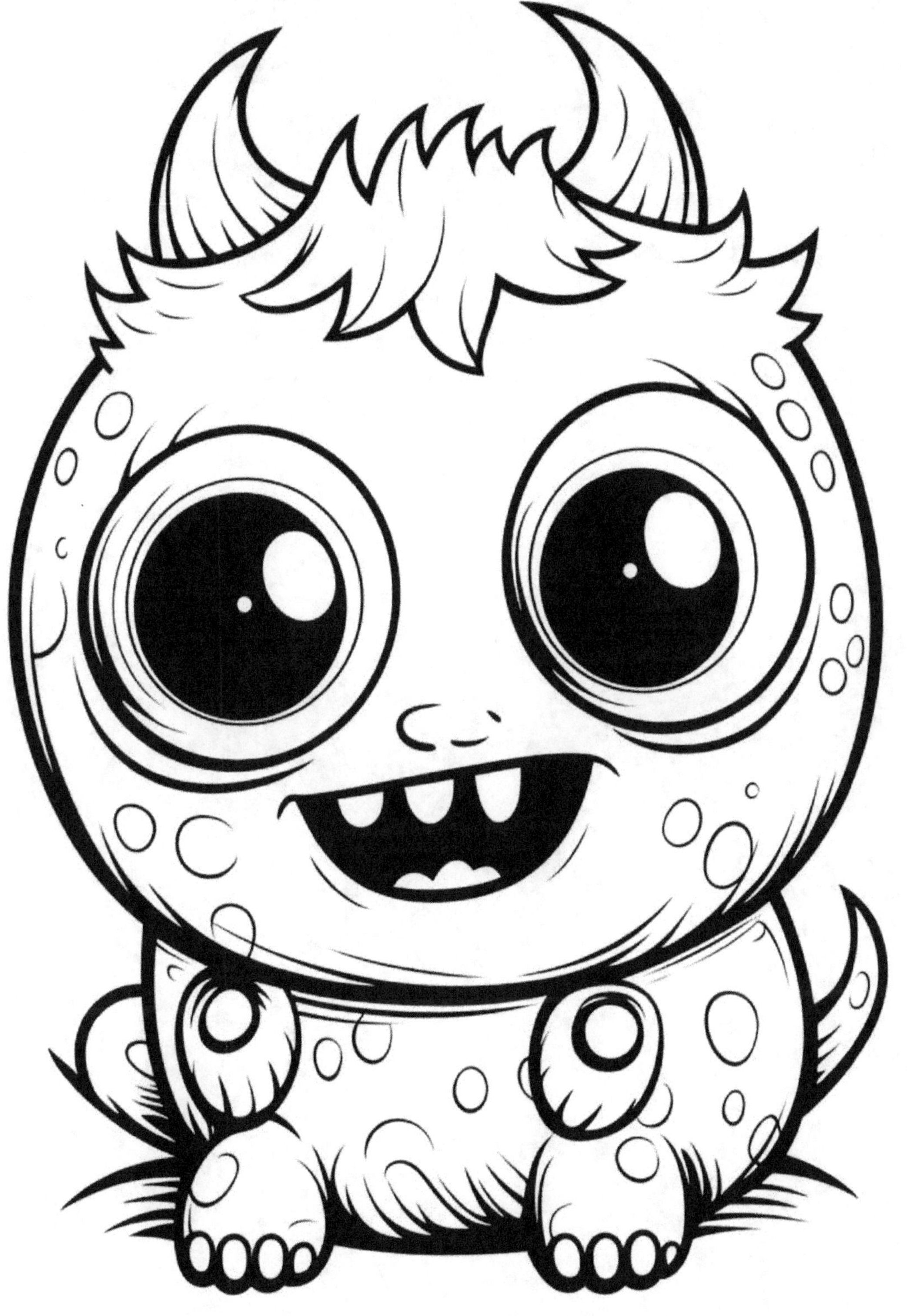

Jollytwirl

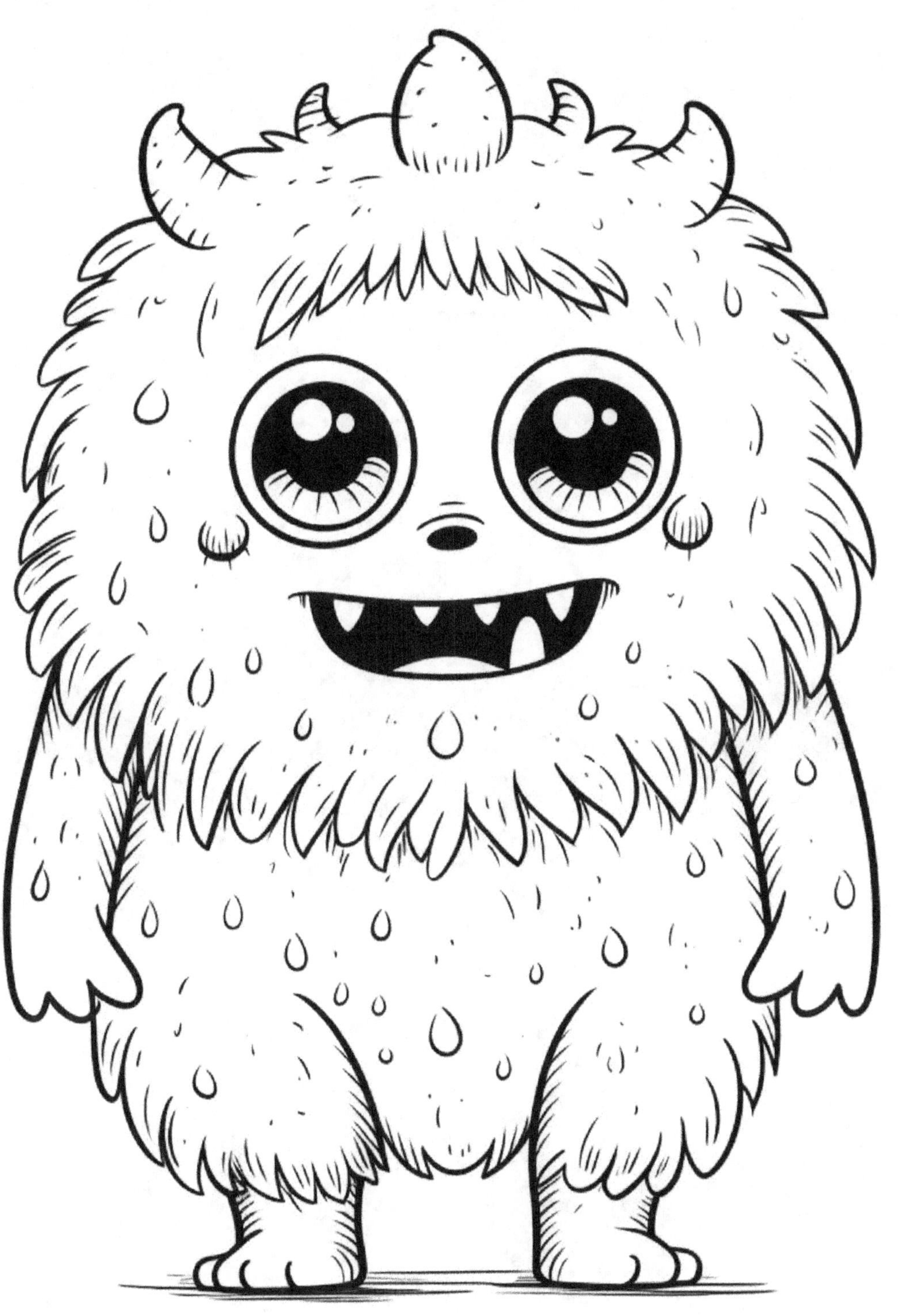

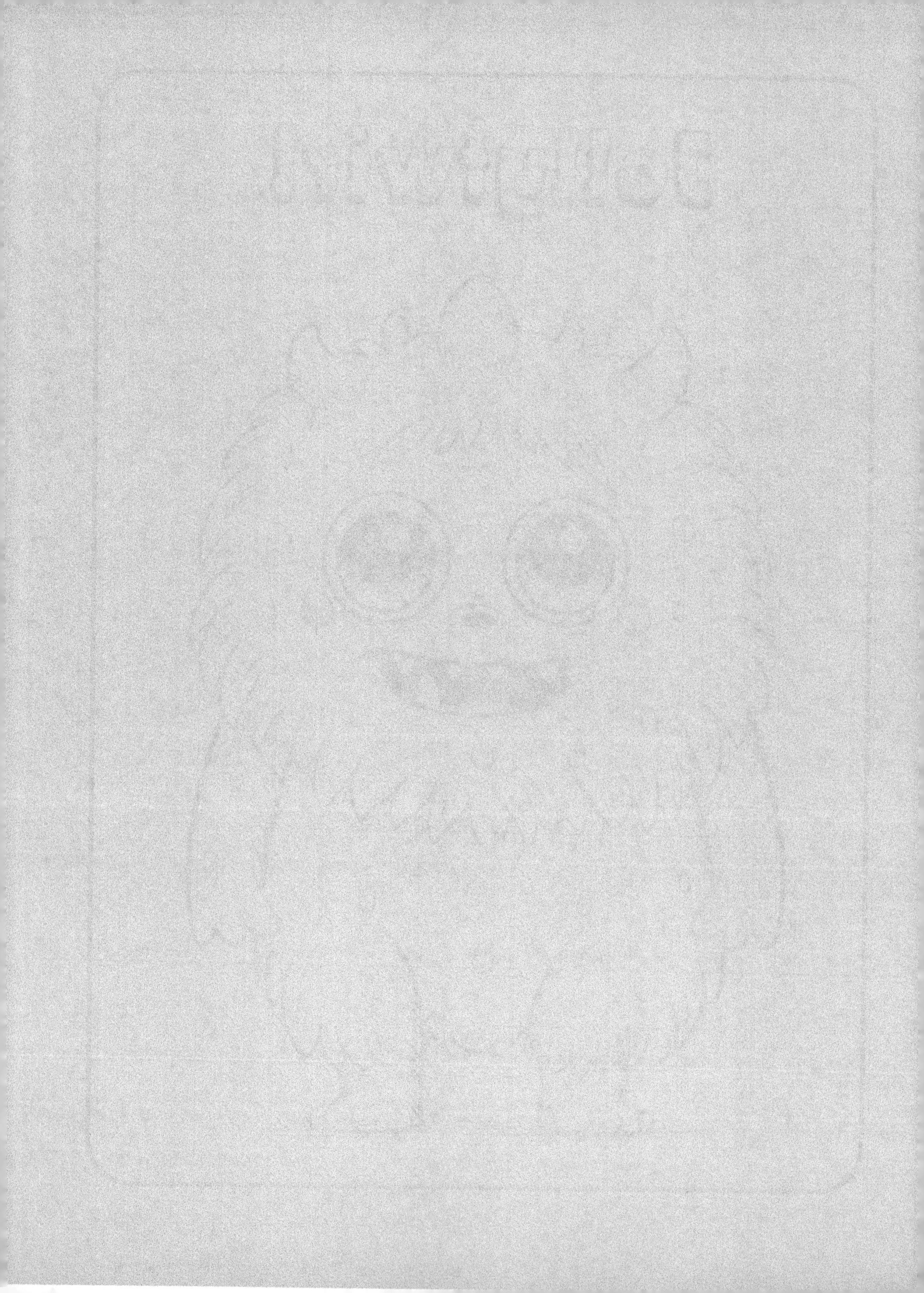

Zigglybop

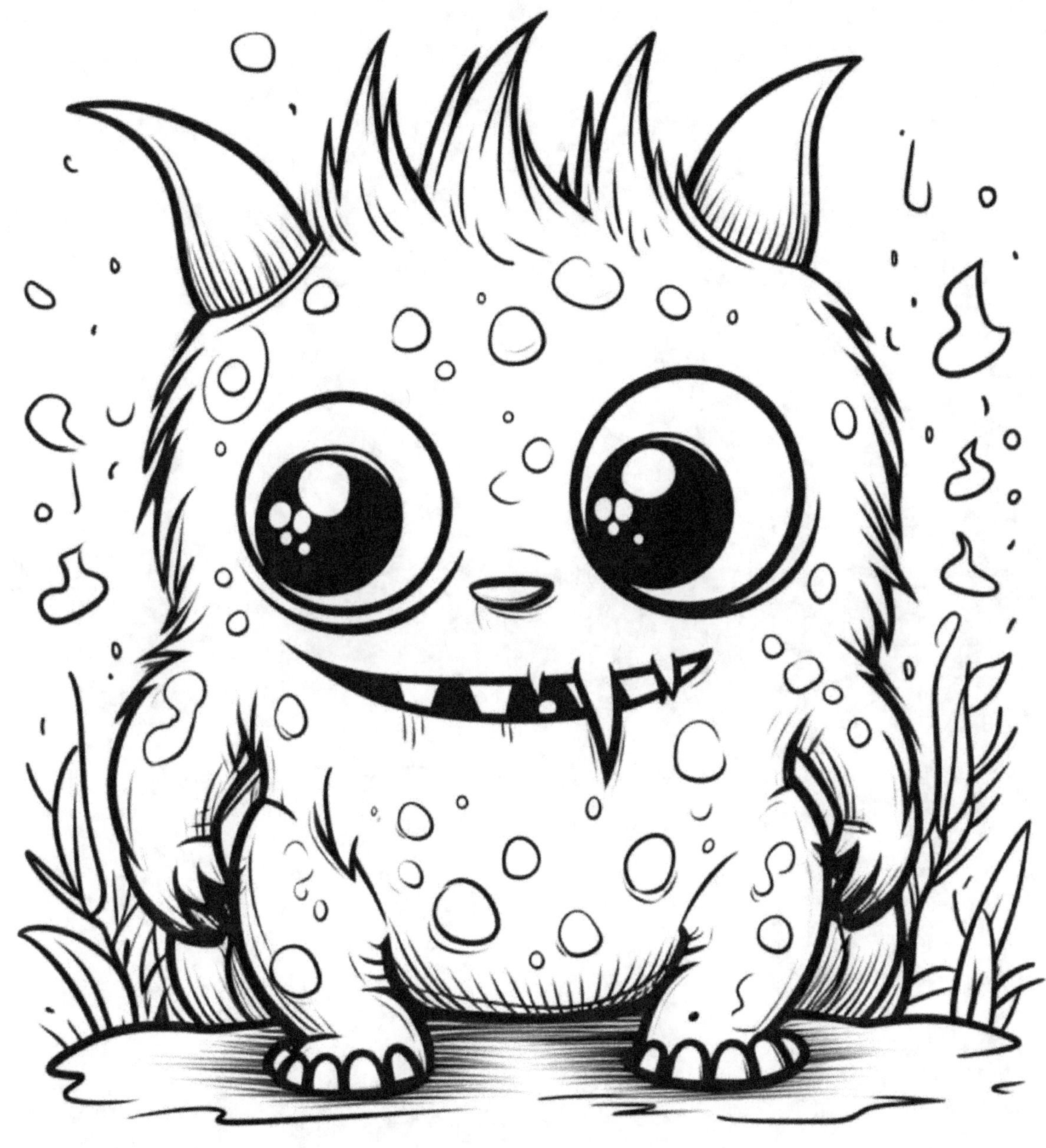

Glimmerfuzz

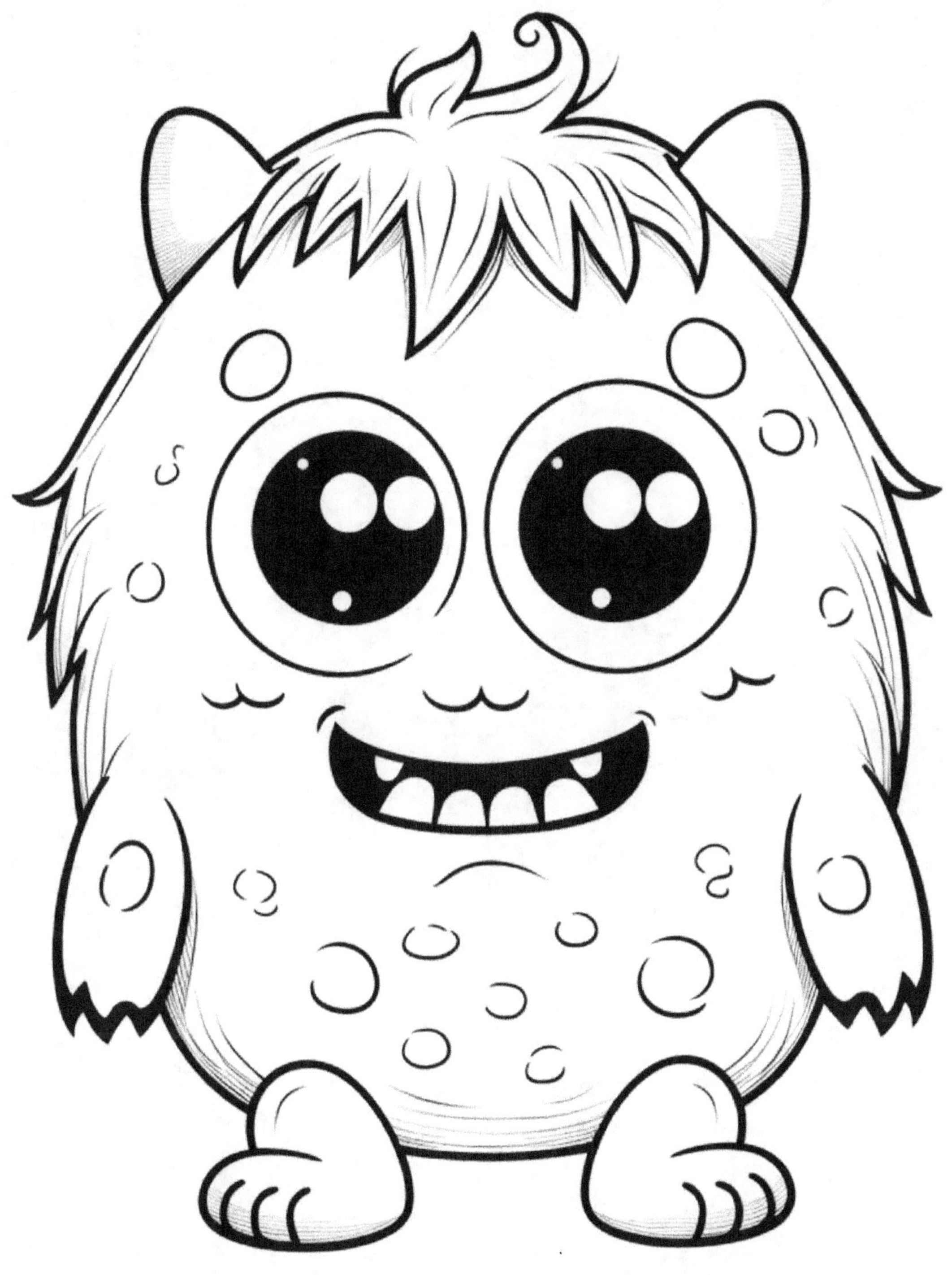

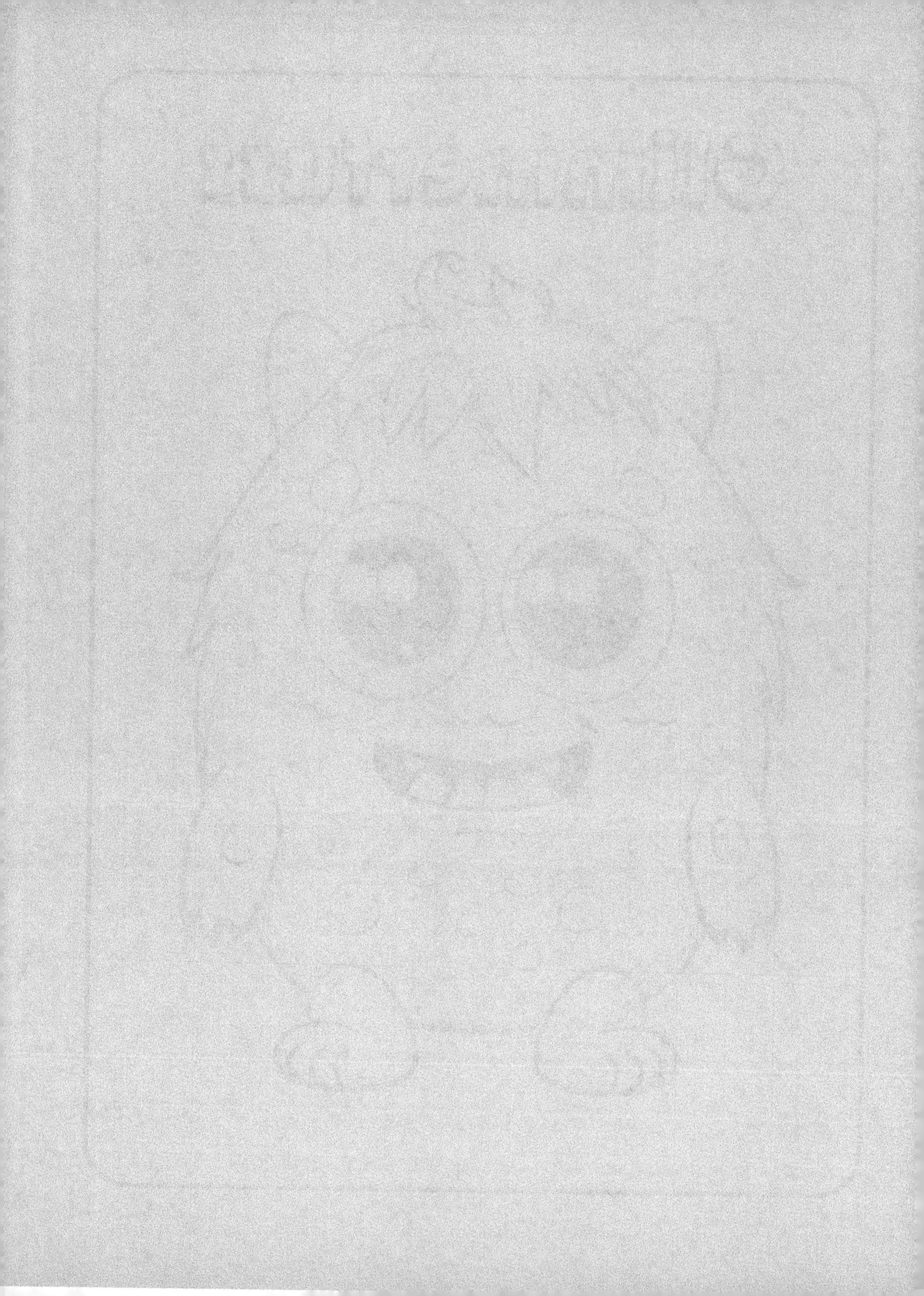

Whiskerwhirl

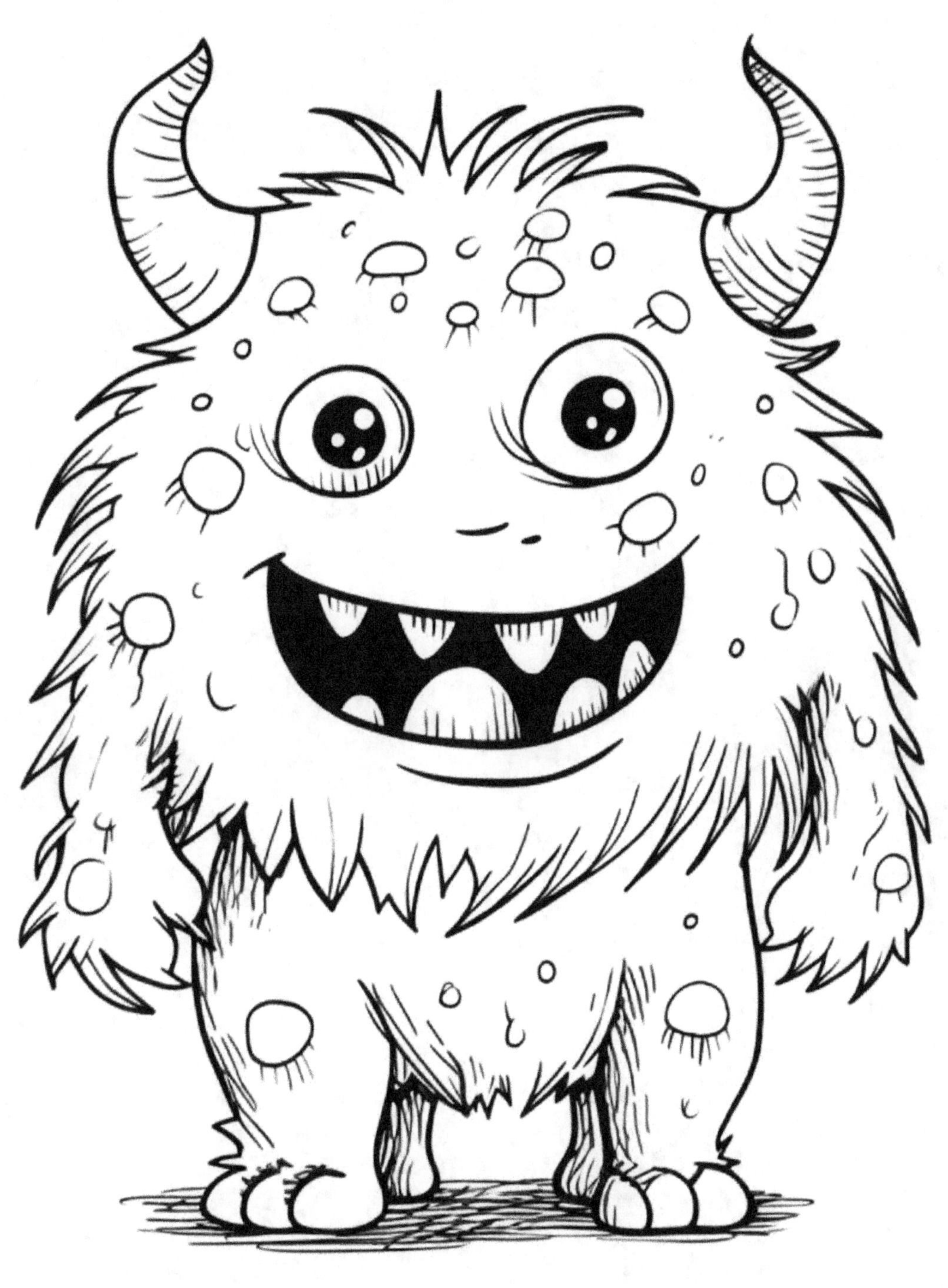